D0975128

Qualatex® presents

Qualatex® presents Balloon Magic®

The Complete Guide to Balloon Figure-Tying

Qualatex® presents

The Complete Guide to Balloon Figure-Tying

by Marvin L. Hardy
Master Magician
and Foremost Authority
on Balloon Sculpture

ISBN: 0-9616600-1-5

PREFACE

Welcome to the fascinating world of Balloon Magic®! With this book (and a little practice) you'll soon be able to create dozens of colorful and lively balloon figures that will delight and entertain people of all ages – including yourself!

The Balloon Magic book is your step-by-step guide to the art of turning long, slender "pencil" balloons into party favors and decorations, accents for floral and balloon arrangements, gifts for children (and the young-at-heart), and storytelling and teaching aids.

This book is designed for the experienced balloon artist, but even those of you who are new to the art can easily follow its directions. I suggest, however, that you first master the basic details and figures at the front of the book before turning to the more difficult instructions later on. If you forget how to do a particular twist or loop needed in a figure, just refer to the index to find the directions you need to review.

Those of you who are left-handed can easily adapt to the directions using the left hand when the right hand is called for.

Once you master the various techniques, you'll be amazed at how easy it is to create balloon figures of your own!

The intricacy of the designs in Balloon Magic call for an extra-durable, full-length balloon. I recommend using only Qualatex® brand 260Q balloons (two inches in diameter and sixty inches long when fully inflated). And to make balloon inflation easy, try the Qualatex Hand Air Inflator. Both products are available from balloon shops and retail stores nationwide.

Now, you're ready for the fun. Of course, you must practice, but that's part of the fun too. Before you know it, you'll be creating the variety of figures in this book – and many of your own as well.

Marvin L. Hardy

Marvin L. Hardy

For best results, store
balloons in plastic, away
from extremes of light
and temperature.

TABLE OF CONTENTS

Inflating 2
Tying 3
Basic Twists 4
Lock Twist 4
Two-Bubble Twist 5
Basic Animal 6
Proportion 7
Mouse 8
Giraffe 10
Bunny Rabbit 12
Adding Detail 14
Floppy Ears 14
Bassett Hound 16
Dachshund 18
Loop Twist 20
Basic Loop Figure 21
Cat 23
Swan 26
Antlers 29
Deer 30
Elk 32
Moose 34
Ram/Bighorn Sheep 36
Loop and Tuck 39
Four-Bubble Twist 40
Poodle 41
Poodle With Ears 43
Monkey 45
Tulip Twist 48
Tulip 50
Daisy 52
Orchid 54
Sunflower 56
Bouquet 59
Pinch Twist 61
Three-Bubble Series with Pinch Twists 63
Chihuahua 64
Squirrel 66
Kangaroo 69
Mane 72
Horse 73
Rocking Horse 76
Lion 79

Lamb 81
Five-Bubble Series with Pinch Twists 83
Five-Bubble Series with Pinch and Pop 85
Teddy Bear 87
Teddy Bear on a Unicycle 90
Three-Bubble Roll Through 93
Love Birds 94
Love Birds in a Swing 97
Parrot in a Swing 101
Dove 104
Eagle 108
Turkey 111
Road Runner 115
Turtle 118
Alligator 120
Frog 123
Bullfrog 126
Fish 130
Kissing Fish 132
Sword 135
Ski Pole 137
Pistol 139
Headphones 141
Skateboard 144
Scooter 147
Chopper 150
Bicycle 154
Airplane 158
Biplane 162
727 Jet 165
Three-Bladed Helicopter 170
Snoopy 176
Woodstock 179
Doll 182
St. Bernard 186
Inflating in the Middle 190
Elephant 191
Unicorn 193
Motorcycle with Kickstand 196
Index 200
About the Author 203

INFLATING

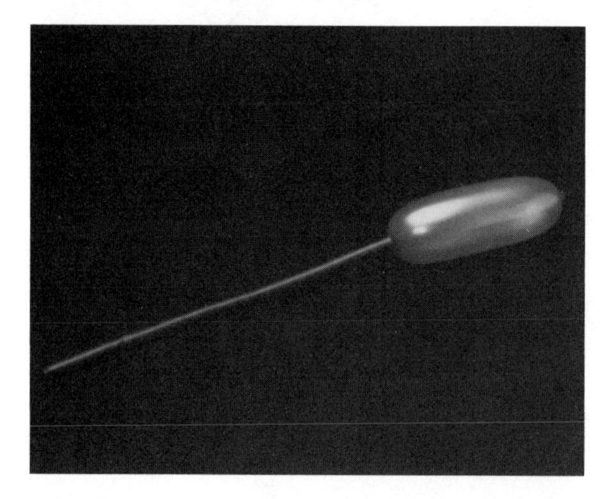

One of the most important things to learn in creating balloon figures is how much to inflate the balloon. Because each twist forces air into the uninflated section, that section must be long enough to accommodate the displaced air.

As a general rule, leave about ½ inch of the balloon uninflated for each twist in the figure. It's natural to overinflate the balloon, so start with less air than you think you'll need. Most figures can be formed with 6-8 inches left uninflated, but practice will teach you how much to inflate for each figure.

You can adjust for too little air in the balloon by reducing the size of some parts of the balloon figure. If there's too much air in the balloon, however, it may pop before you complete the figure.

HINT: For easy tying, hold the balloon about an inch from the lip end while inflating to prevent inflation of that section of the balloon.

TYING

Many people find it difficult to tie a balloon. Although any method that works for you is acceptable, this is the one I've found to be the simplest.

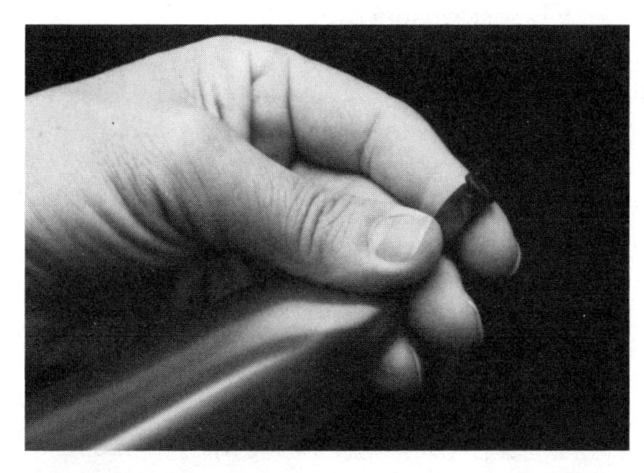

1 Hold the lip end of the inflated balloon between the thumb and the side of the middle finger of the left hand with the lip of the balloon pointing up.

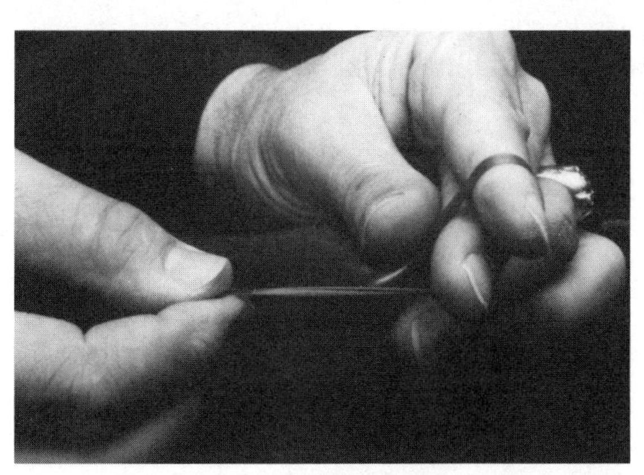

2 Grasp the lip between the thumb and the pointer finger of the right hand. Stretch the balloon out and wrap it clockwise around the tips of the pointer and middle fingers of the left hand.

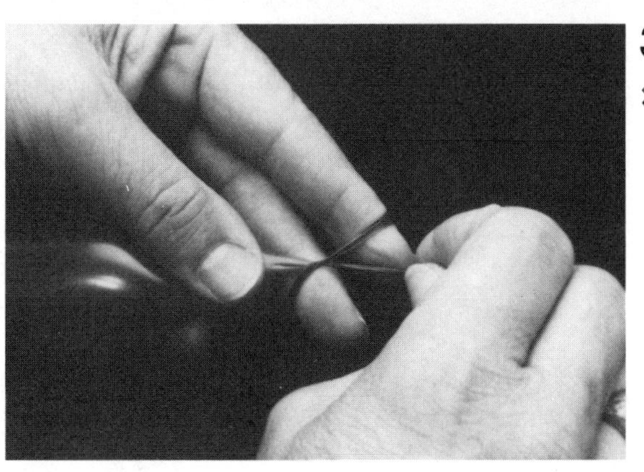

3 With the fingers of your left hand spread, tuck the lip down and between your left pointer and middle fingers, then up and through the loop the balloon forms around them. Grasp the lip again after it passes through the loop and continue to hold it while slipping the left fingers from the loop.

BASIC TWISTS

There are several twists and bubble formations that are common to many figures. Among the most basic of these are the lock twist and two-bubble twist.

HINT: When making twists and bubble formations, pinch the balloon slightly with the left hand while twisting it with the right (vice versa if you're left-handed). Always twist the uninflated end (rather than the knot end) while holding the knot end stationary, and always twist the balloon in the same direction.

LOCK TWIST

Each series of bubbles must be held in place by a lock twist to keep it from untwisting. A lock twist is made by twisting together two bubbles at the base – or the ends of one bubble (making a Loop Twist – see page 20).

HINT: When lock twisting, slightly pull the bubbles apart to help reduce friction between the bubbles and lessen the chance of popping them.

TWO-BUBBLE TWIST

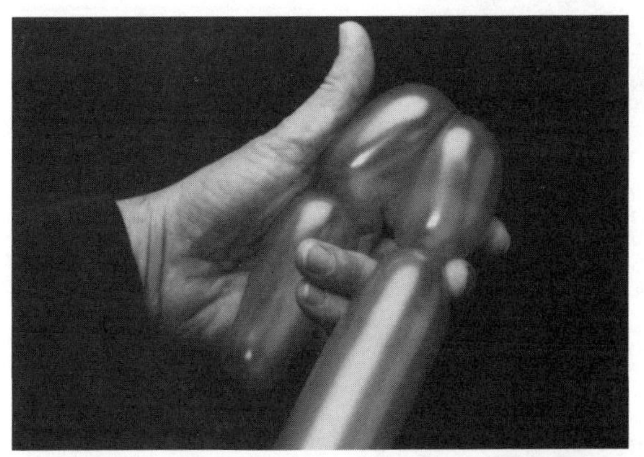

1 Hold the inflated balloon in your left hand with the uninflated end pointing right. Form an initial bubble, followed by a bubble of the desired length. Form a third bubble equal in length to the second bubble.

2 Lock twist these two bubbles at the base.

BASIC ANIMAL

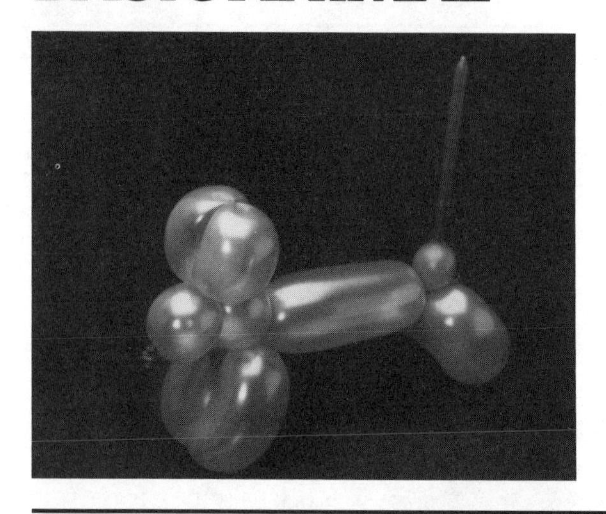

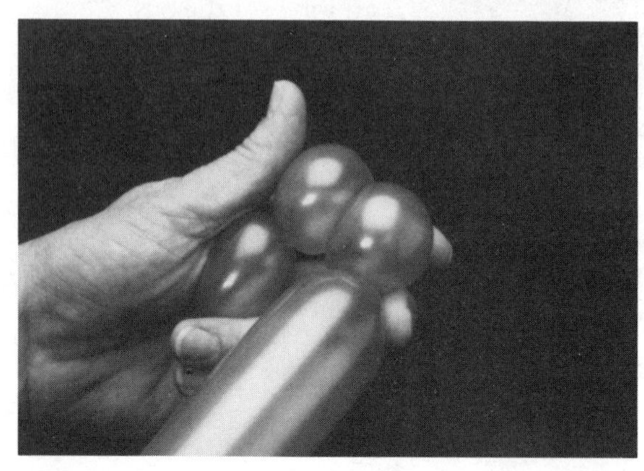

1 Inflate the balloon, leaving an 8-inch uninflated end. Tie a knot. Hold the balloon in your left hand with the uninflated end pointing right. To make the head and ears, form three 1-inch bubbles.

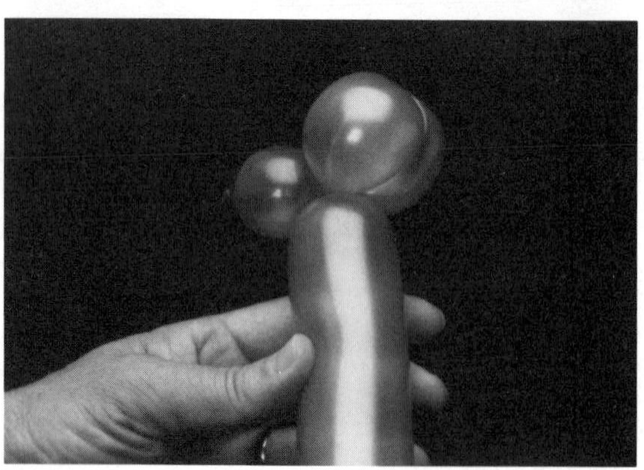

2 Lock twist the last two 1-inch bubbles at the base to complete the ears.

3 Form a 1-inch bubble for the neck. To make the front legs, form two 2-inch bubbles and lock twist them at the base.

4 Form a 3-inch bubble for the body. To make the back legs, form two 2-inch bubbles and lock twist them at the base. Leave a small bubble of air at the base of the tail to hold the back legs in place and complete the figure.

PROPORTION

Most animals are similar in structure, with a head, neck, legs, torso, and usually a tail. Any basic animal figure can be easily made by adding the twists outlined in the previous figure and changing the proportion or size of the bubbles. A rabbit, for example, has long ears, a short neck, short front legs, long back legs, and a short tail. A giraffe has short ears, a long neck, long front legs, shorter back legs, and a long tail. A mouse is small in every detail.

MOUSE

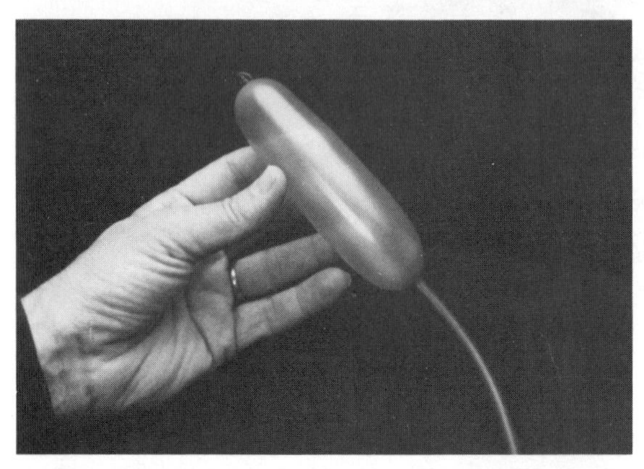

1 Inflate the balloon to form a 5-inch bubble. Tie a knot.

2 Hold the balloon in your left hand with the uninflated end pointing right. To make the head and ears, form three 1-inch bubbles. Lock twist the last two bubbles at the base to complete the ears.

3 Form a ½-inch bubble for the neck. To make the front legs, form two 1-inch bubbles and lock twist them at the base.

4 To make the body and back legs, form three 1-inch bubbles. Lock twist the last two bubbles at the base to complete the back legs. Leave a small bubble of air at the base of the tail to hold the back legs in place and complete the figure.

GIRAFFE

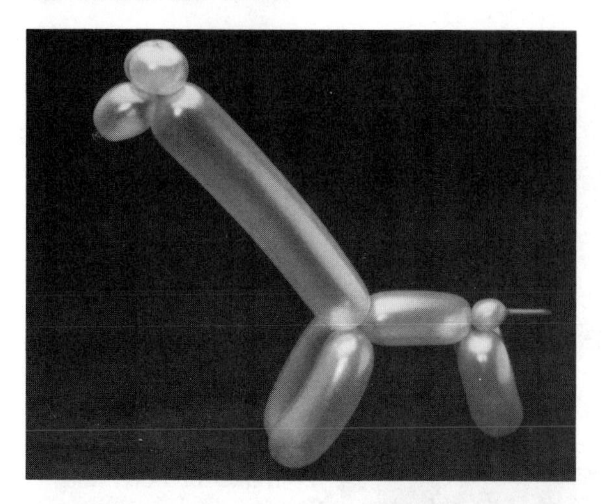

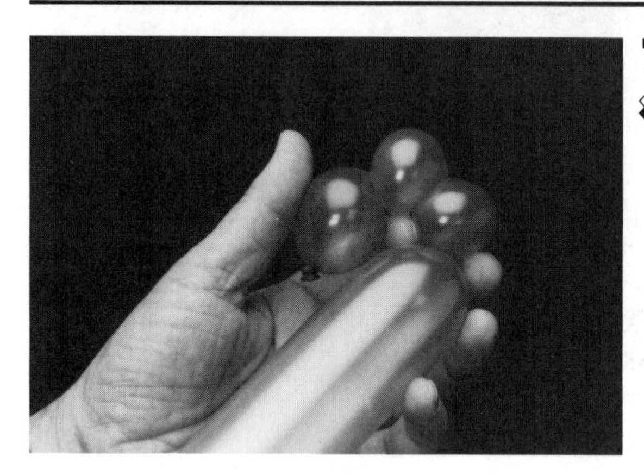

1 Inflate the balloon, leaving a 4-inch uninflated end. Tie a knot. Hold the balloon in your left hand with the uninflated end pointing right. To make the head and ears, form three 1-inch bubbles. Lock twist the last two bubbles at the base to complete the ears.

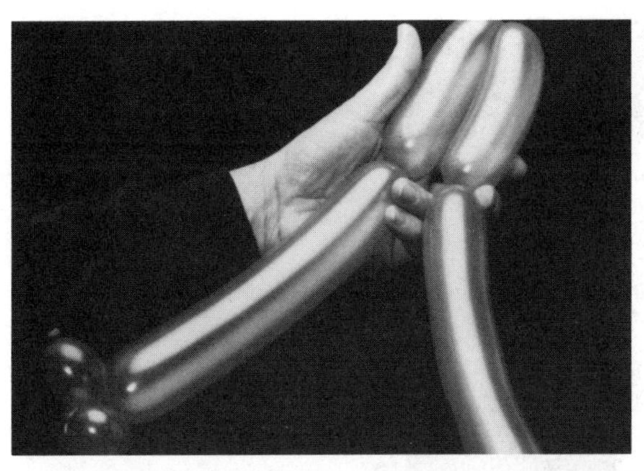

2 Form an 8-inch bubble for the neck. To make the front legs, form two 4-inch bubbles and lock twist them at the base.

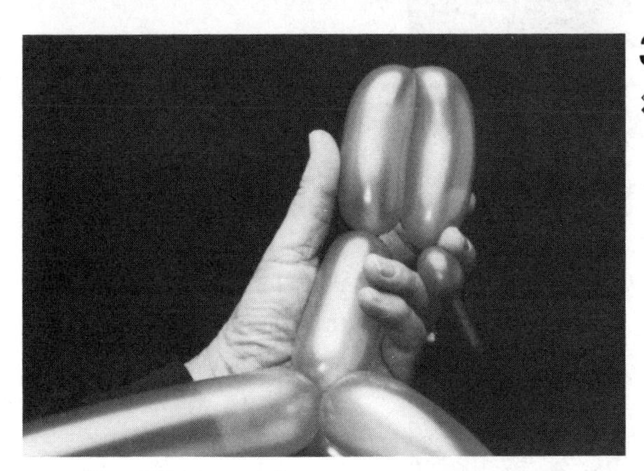

3 To make the body and back legs, form three 3-inch bubbles. Lock twist the last two bubbles at the base. Leave a small bubble of air at the base of the tail to hold the back legs in place and complete the figure.

BUNNY RABBIT

1 Inflate the balloon, leaving a 3-inch uninflated end. Tie a knot. Hold the balloon in your left hand with the uninflated end pointing right. Form a 1-inch bubble for the head. To make the ears, form two 3-inch bubbles and lock twist them at the base.

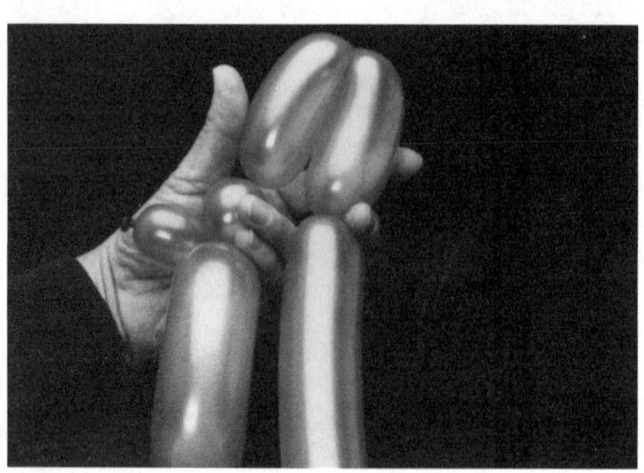

2 Form a 1-inch bubble for the neck. To make the front legs, form two 2-inch bubbles and lock twist them at the base.

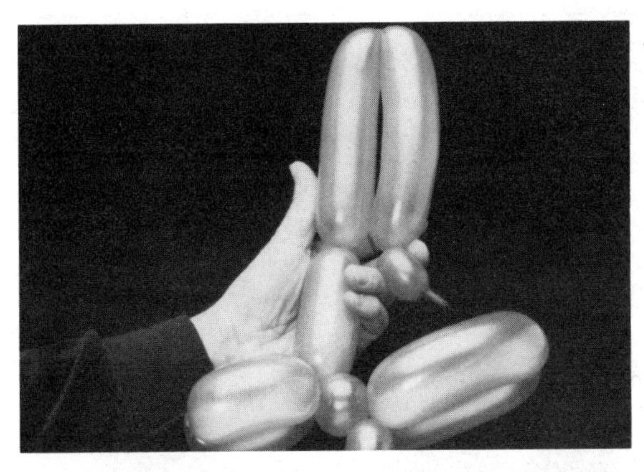

3 Form a 3-inch bubble for the body. To make the back legs, form two 4-inch bubbles and lock twist them at the base. Leave a small bubble of air at the base of the tail to hold the back legs in place and complete the figure.

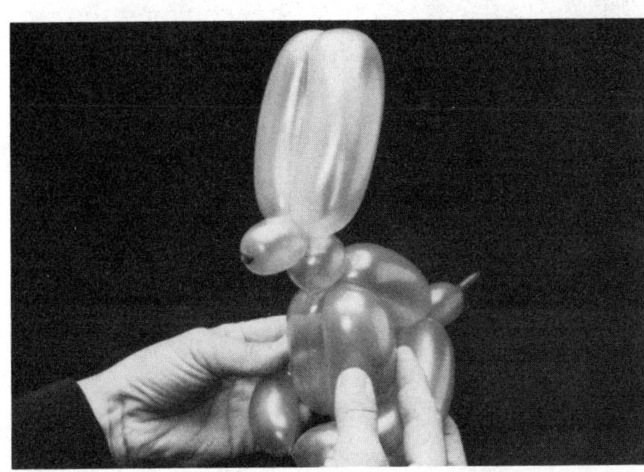

4 To place the figure in a sitting position, tuck the front legs between the back legs.

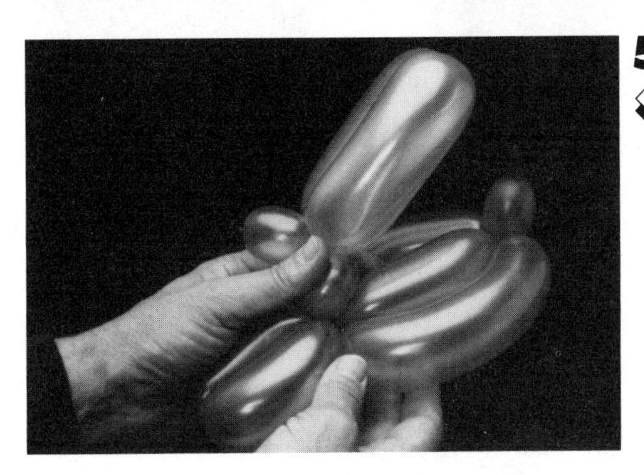

5 To place the figure in a reclining position, wedge the body between the back legs with the front legs extended forward.

ADDING DETAIL

Many animal figures can be formed easily and quickly by using only the basic twists described on the preceding pages. But you can add unique details to these figures by using the twists and bubble formations shown on the following pages.

FLOPPY EARS

Long, floppy ears, common to many animals, can be created using the following balloon figure detail.

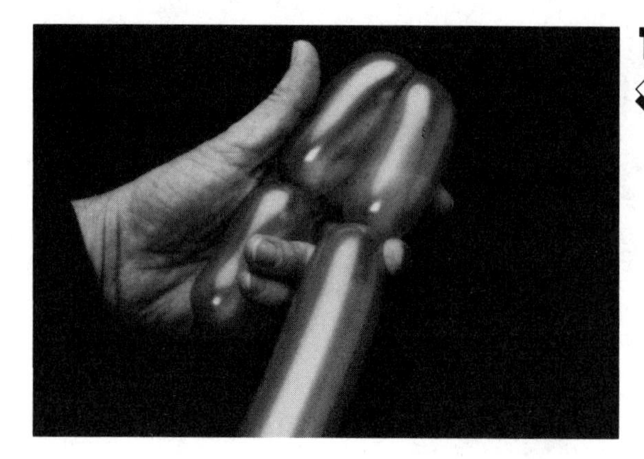

1 Begin by holding the inflated balloon in your left hand with the uninflated end pointing right. To make the head and ears, form three 2-inch bubbles. Lock twist the last two bubbles at the base to complete the ears.

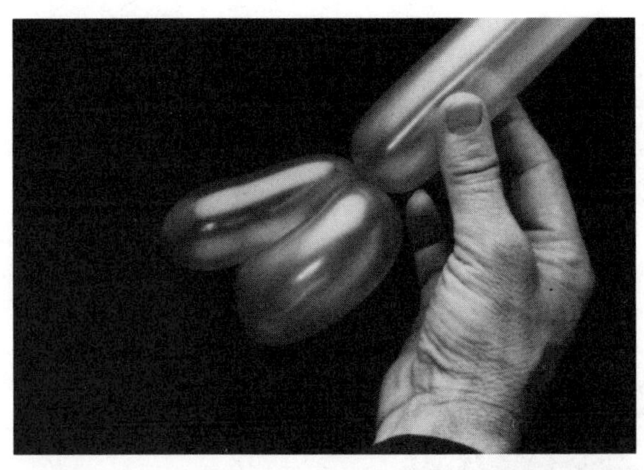

2 Turn the balloon so the ears point down. Wedge the head between the two ears so it also points down.

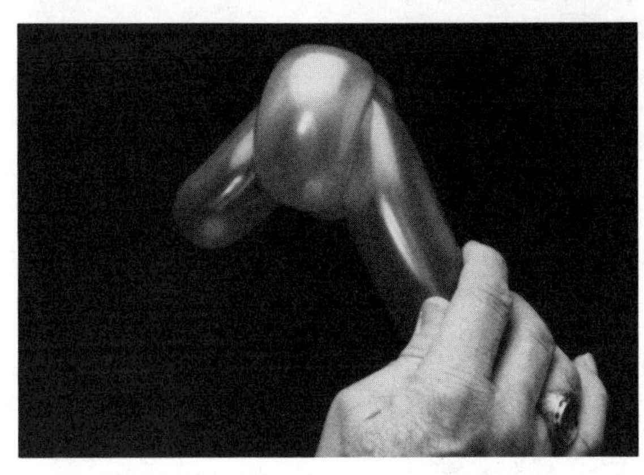

3 To complete the detail, wedge the inflated portion of the balloon between the ears and opposite the head, so it also points down.

BASSETT HOUND

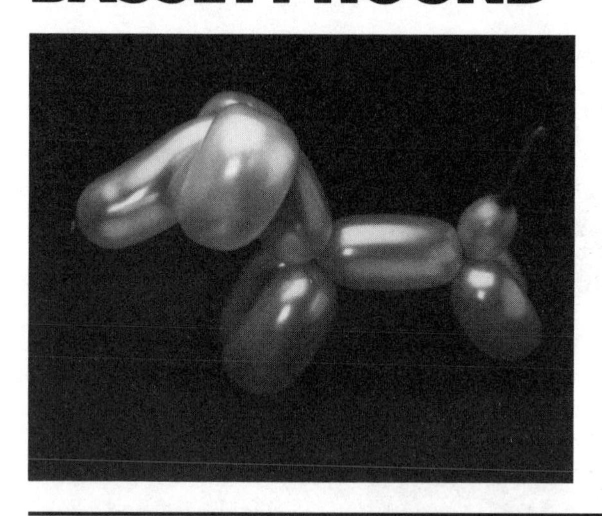

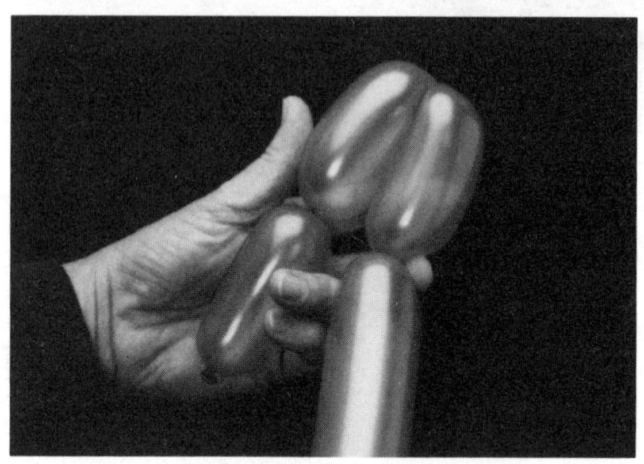

1 Inflate the balloon, leaving a 6-inch uninflated end. Tie a knot. Hold the balloon in your left hand with the uninflated end pointing right. To make the head and ears, form three 2-inch bubbles. Lock twist the last two bubbles at the base to complete the ears.

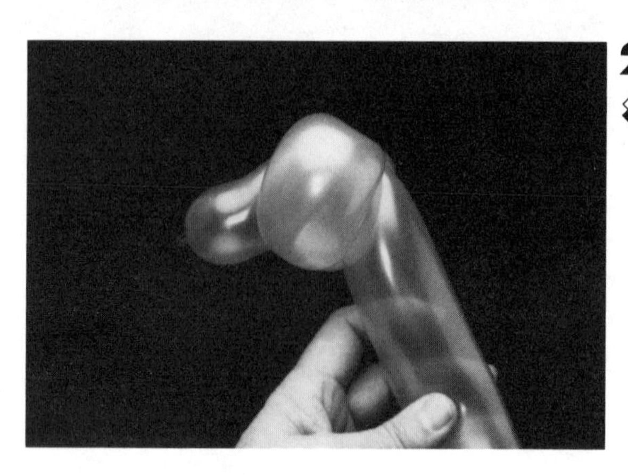

2 Turn the balloon so the ears point down. To complete the head, wedge the head and neck bubbles between the ears so they both point down.

3 To make the neck and front legs, form three 2-inch bubbles. Lock twist the last two at the base to complete the front legs.

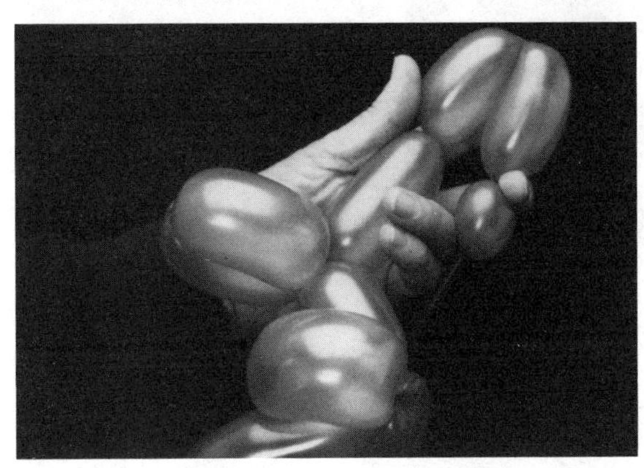

4 Form a 3-inch bubble for the body. To make the back legs, form two 2-inch bubbles and lock twist them at the base. Leave a small bubble of air at the base of the tail to hold the back legs in place and complete the figure.

DACHSHUND

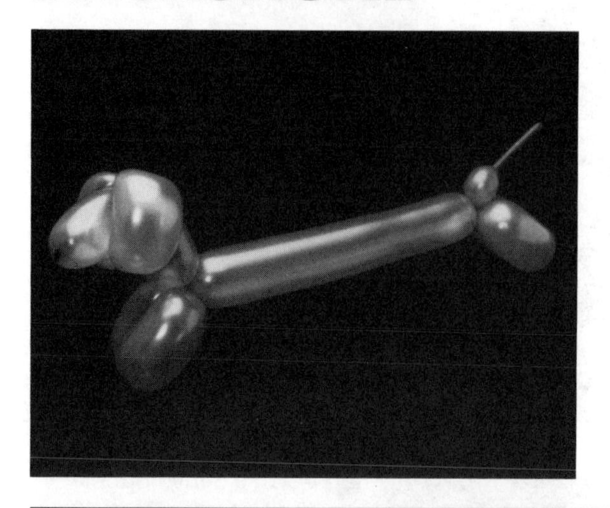

1 Inflate the balloon, leaving a 6-inch uninflated end. Tie a knot. Hold the balloon in your left hand with the uninflated end pointing right. To make the head and ears, form three 1½-inch bubbles. Lock twist the last two bubbles at the base to complete the ears.

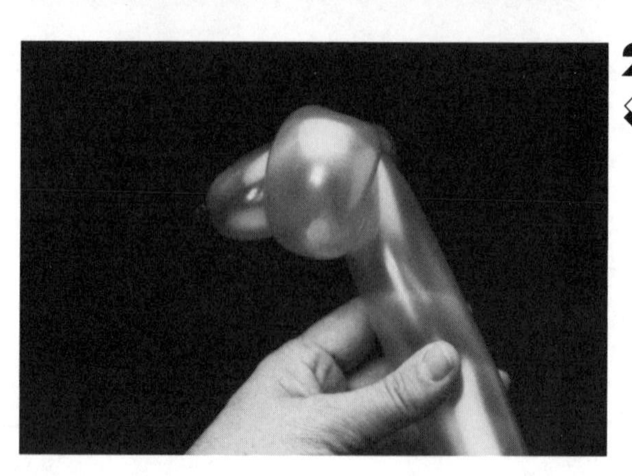

2 Turn the balloon so the ears point down. To complete the head, wedge the head and neck bubbles between the ears so they both point down.

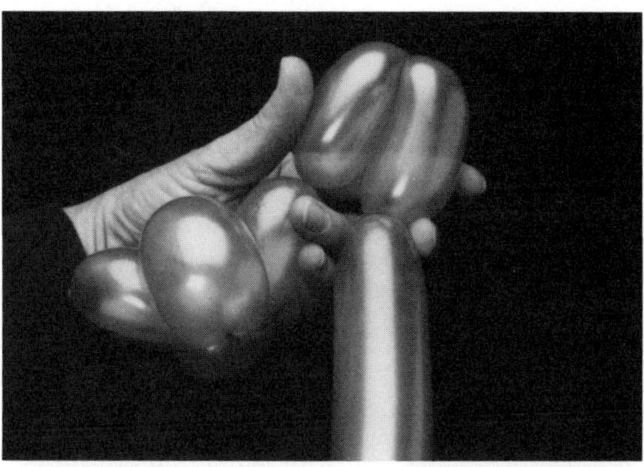

3 To make the neck and front legs, form three 1½-inch bubbles. Lock twist the last two at the base to complete the front legs.

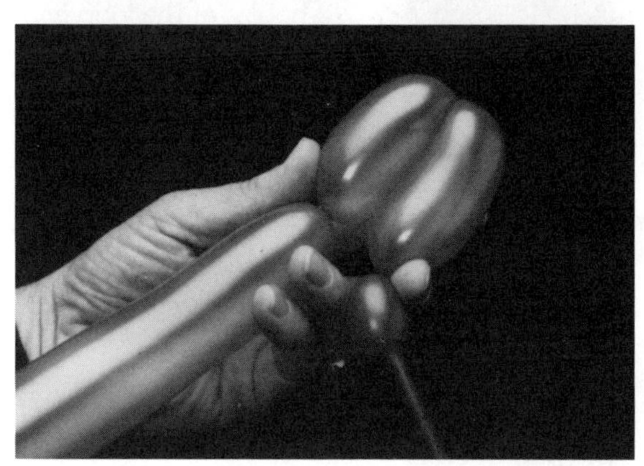

4 Form an 8-inch bubble for the body. To make the back legs, form two 1½-inch bubbles and lock twist them at the base. Leave a small bubble of air at the base of the tail to hold the back legs in place and complete the figure.

LOOP TWIST

The loop twist is used to form simple ears and legs, the petals of flowers, the back legs of animals that stand erect (such as the bear), the feet of some birds, the handguards of the sword, and the wings and rudders of aircraft.

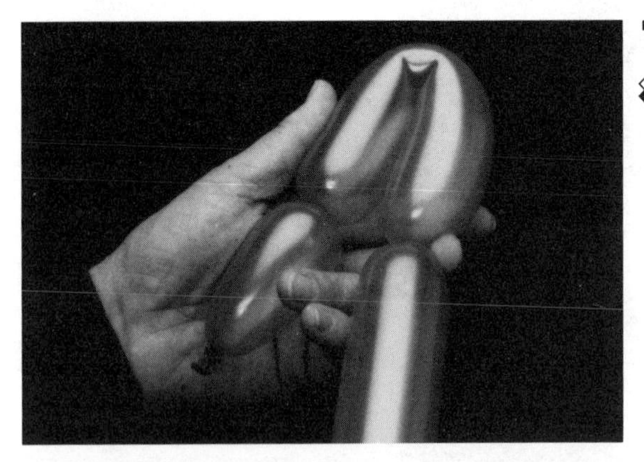

1 Hold the inflated balloon in your left hand with the uninflated end pointing right. Form a bubble. To make a loop, fold the balloon in equal halves, after the initial bubble. (The size of the loop is measured from the twist at its base to its outer top edge.)

2 Twist the balloon at the end of the loop where both sides are equal, then lock twist the ends.

BASIC LOOP FIGURE

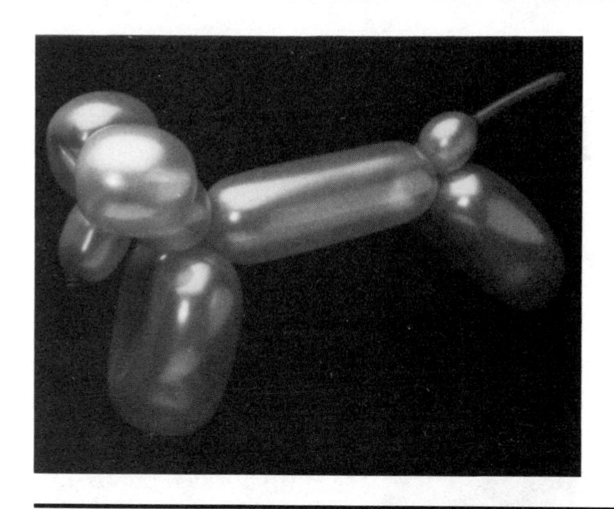

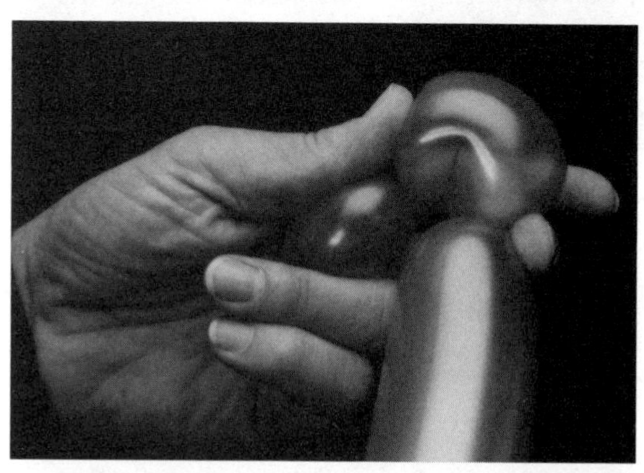

1 Inflate the balloon, leaving an 8-inch uninflated end. Tie a knot. Hold the balloon in your left hand with the uninflated end pointing right. To make the head, form a 1-inch bubble. To make one ear, form a 1-inch loop.

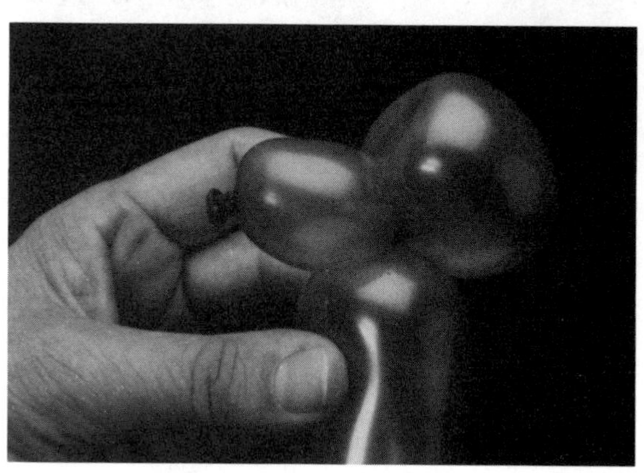

2 Lock twist the ends of the loop to complete that ear.

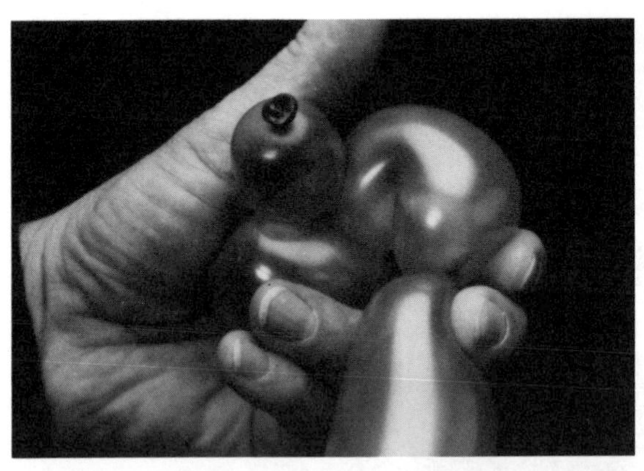

3 To make the other ear, form a 1-inch loop and lock twist the ends.

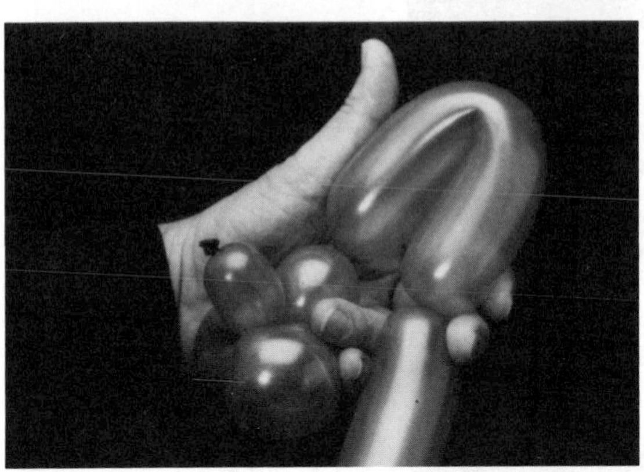

4 Form a 1-inch bubble for the neck. To make the front legs, form a 4-inch loop and lock twist the ends.

5 Form a 4-inch bubble for the body. To make the back legs, form a 4-inch loop and lock twist the ends. Leave a small bubble of air at the base of the tail to hold the back legs in place and complete the figure.

CAT

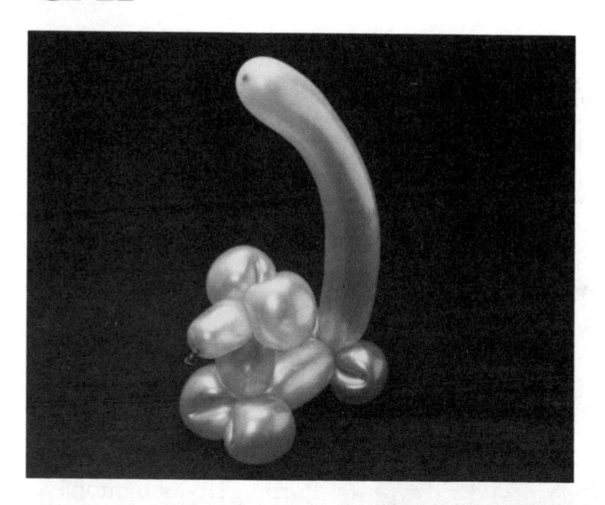

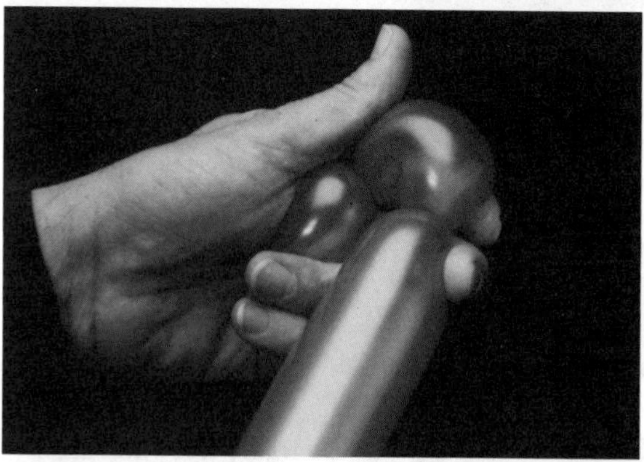

1 Inflate the balloon, leaving a 6-inch uninflated end. Tie a knot. Hold the balloon in your left hand with the uninflated end pointing right. To make the head, form a 1-inch bubble. To make one ear, form a 1-inch loop.

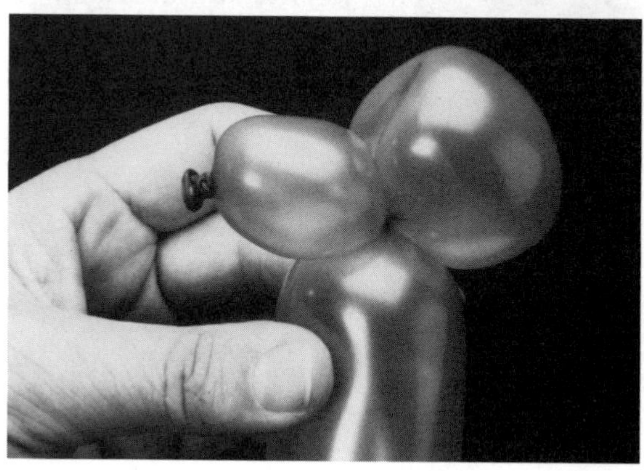

2 Lock twist the ends of the loop to complete that ear.

3 To make the other ear, form a 1-inch loop and lock twist the ends.

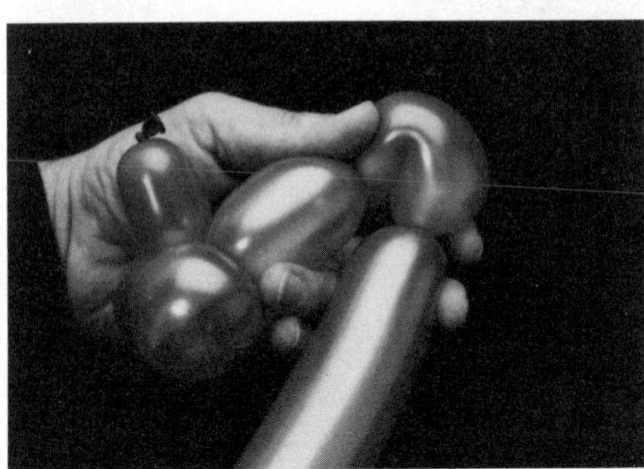

4 Form a 1½-inch bubble for the neck. To make one front leg, form a 1-inch loop and lock twist the ends.

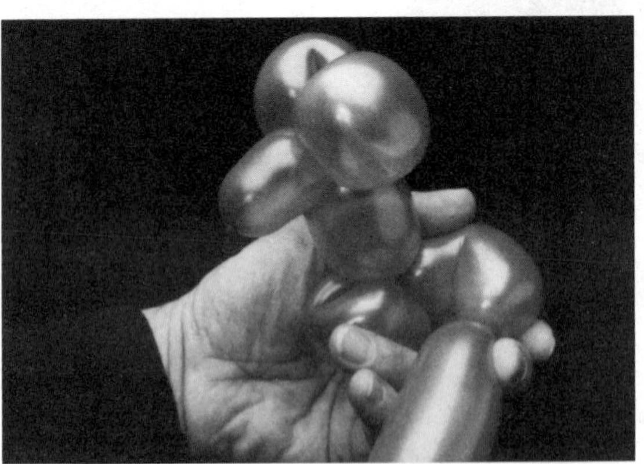

5 To make the other front leg, form a 1-inch loop and lock twist the ends.

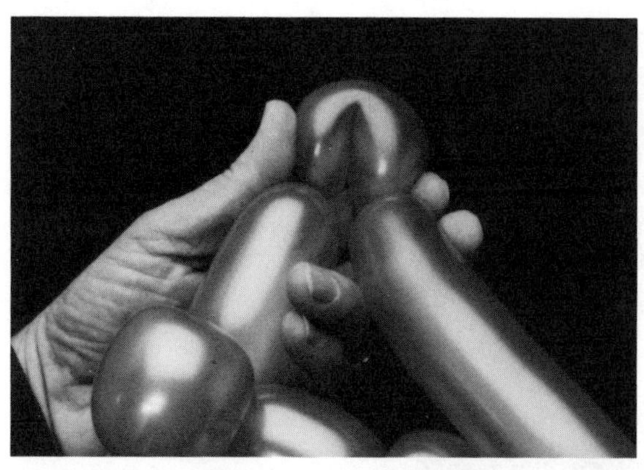

6 Form a 3-inch bubble for the body. To make one back leg, form a 1-inch loop and lock twist the ends.

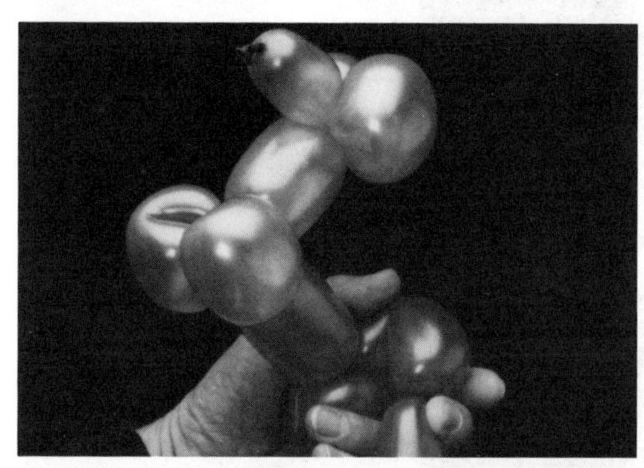

7 To make the other back leg, form a 1-inch loop and lock twist the ends.

8 Curve the tail up over the body to complete the figure.

SWAN

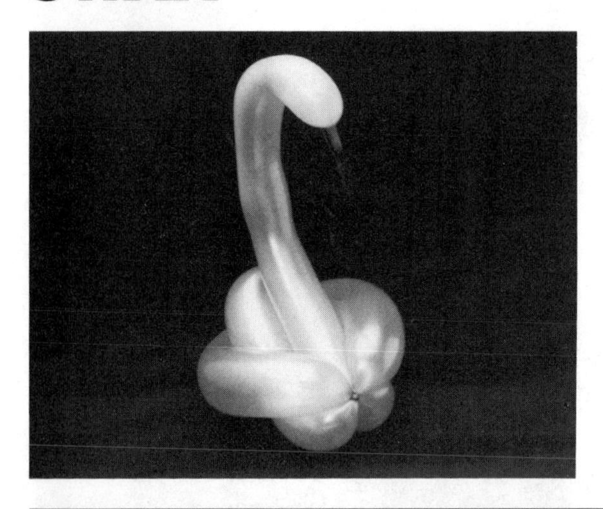

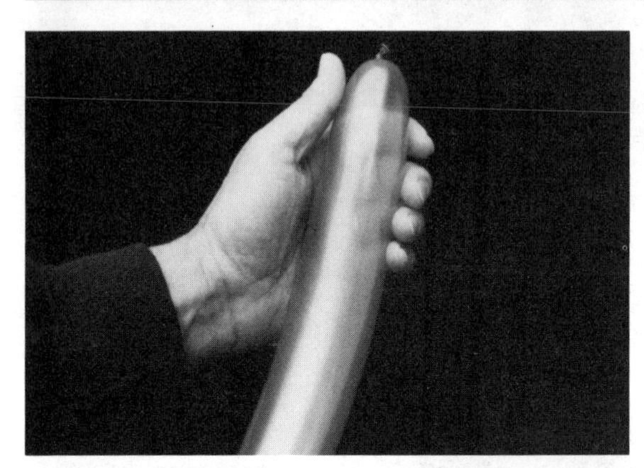

1 Inflate the balloon, leaving a 3-inch uninflated end. Tie a knot. Hold the balloon in your left hand with the uninflated end pointing down.

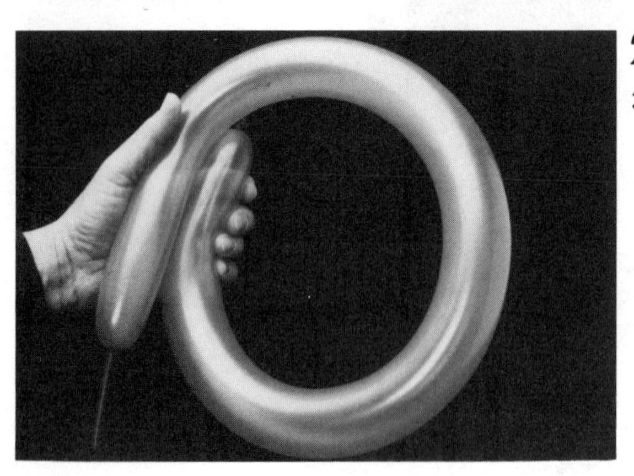

2 Bring the uninflated end up and around to form a loop. The two ends of the balloon should overlap about 6 inches.

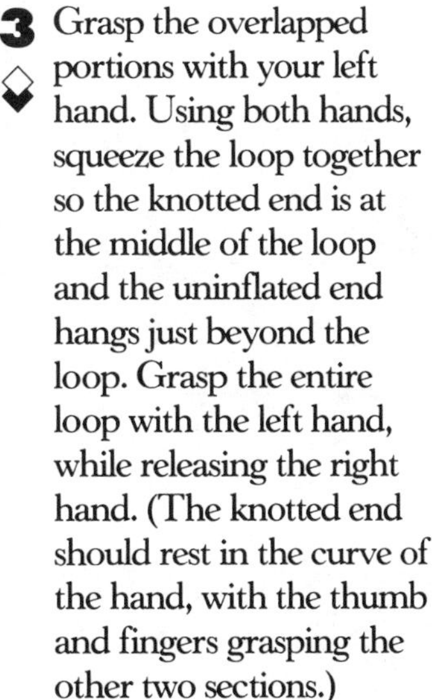

3 Grasp the overlapped portions with your left hand. Using both hands, squeeze the loop together so the knotted end is at the middle of the loop and the uninflated end hangs just beyond the loop. Grasp the entire loop with the left hand, while releasing the right hand. (The knotted end should rest in the curve of the hand, with the thumb and fingers grasping the other two sections.)

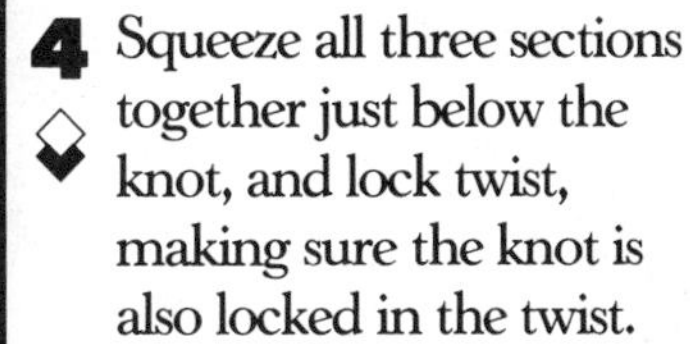

4 Squeeze all three sections together just below the knot, and lock twist, making sure the knot is also locked in the twist.

5 To make the body and tail, tuck one of the loops through the other.

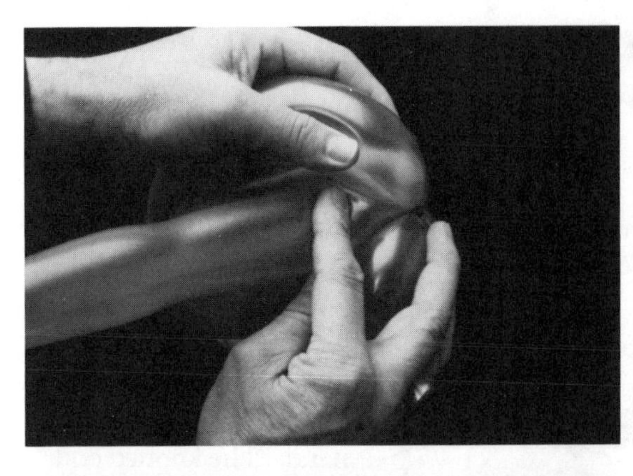

6 To make the neck and hold it upright, wedge the base of the uninflated portion between the ends of the outer loop.

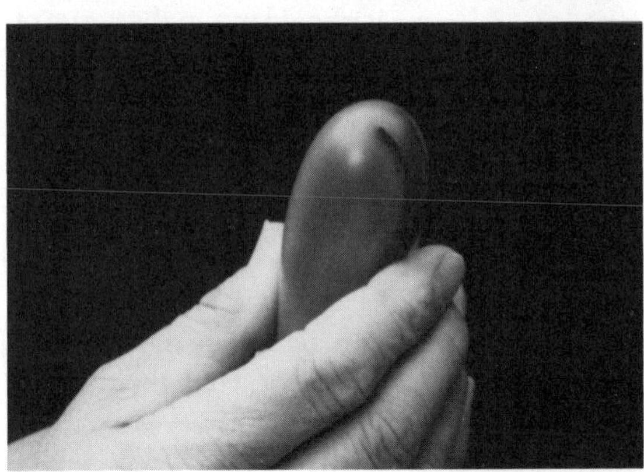

7 To make the head and beak, fold the uninflated tip down along the front of the neck and hold it at the end with your pointer finger.

8 Grasp the neck at this point with both hands and squeeze it, forcing air into the uninflated tip.

ANTLERS

Antlers can be formed by adding bubbles to a standard two-bubble ear assembly.

1 Hold the balloon in your left hand with the uninflated end pointing right. To make the head and one side of the antlers, form a 1-inch bubble and a chain of four ½-inch bubbles. Lock twist the first and last ½-inch bubbles at the base.

2 To make the other side of the antlers, form a chain of four ½-inch bubbles and lock twist the first and last bubbles at the base.

3 The broad antlers of a moose can be made by using two 1½-inch bubbles instead of four ½-inch bubbles.

The following animals are made with several different variations of antlers and horns.

DEER

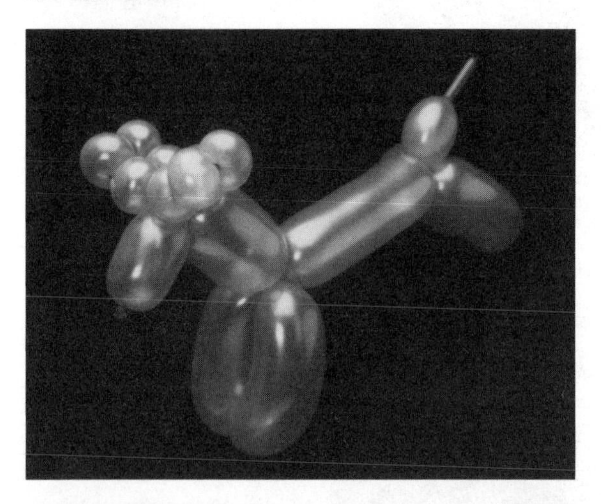

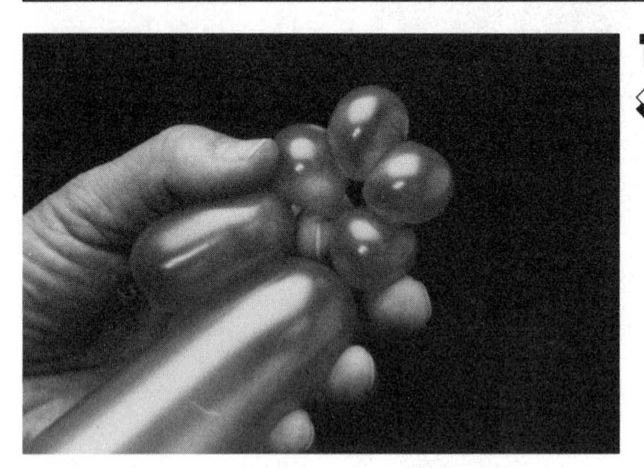

1 Inflate the balloon, leaving an 8-inch uninflated end. Tie a knot. Hold the balloon in your left hand with the uninflated end pointing right. Form a 1-inch bubble for the head. To make one side of the antlers, form four ½-inch bubbles and lock twist the first and last bubbles at the base.

2 To make the other side of the antlers, form four ½-inch bubbles and lock twist the first and last bubbles at the base.

3 Form a 2-inch bubble for the neck. To make the front legs, form two 3-inch bubbles and lock twist them at the base.

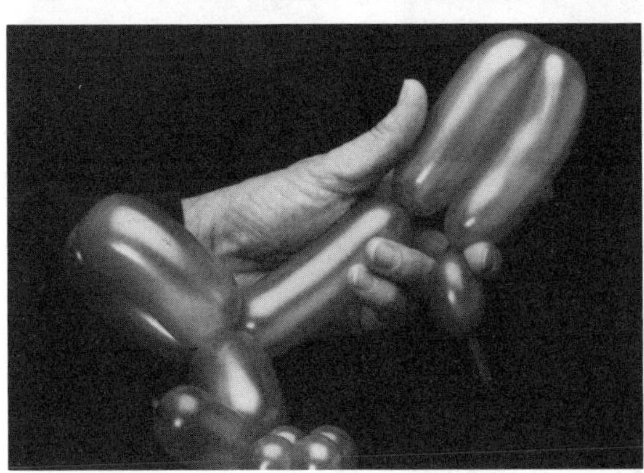

4 To make the body and back legs, form three 3-inch bubbles. Lock twist the last two at the base to complete the back legs. Leave a small bubble of air at the base of the tail to hold the back legs in place and complete the figure.

ELK

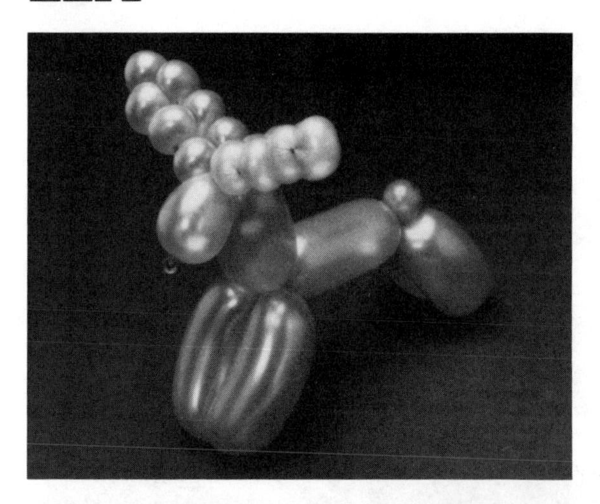

1 Inflate the balloon, leaving an 8-inch uninflated end. Tie a knot. Hold the balloon in your left hand with the uninflated end pointing right. Form a 1-inch bubble for the head. To make one side of the antlers, form a chain of seven ½-inch bubbles.

2 Lock twist the first and last bubbles of the chain at the base, forming a loop. To complete that side of the antlers, lock twist the third and fifth bubbles of the chain.

3 To make the other side of the antlers, form another chain of seven ½-inch bubbles. Lock twist the first and last bubbles of the chain, forming a loop. Complete the antlers by lock twisting the third and fifth bubbles.

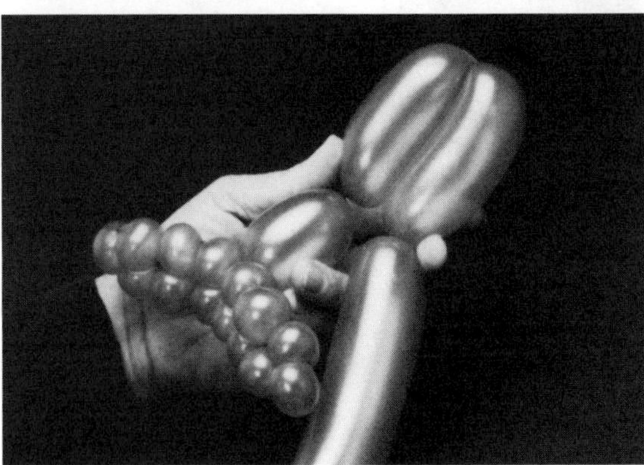

4 Form a 2-inch bubble for the neck. To make the front legs, form two 3-inch bubbles and lock twist them at the base.

5 To make the body and back legs, form three 3-inch bubbles. Lock twist the last two at the base to complete the back legs. Leave a small bubble of air at the base of the tail to hold the back legs in place and complete the figure.

MOOSE

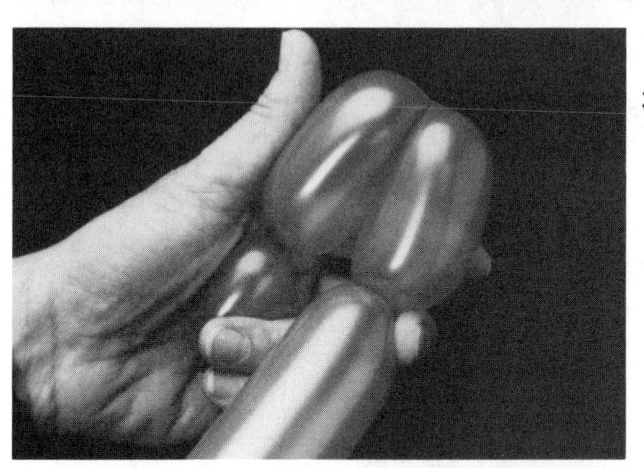

1 Inflate the balloon, leaving a 6-inch uninflated end. Tie a knot. Hold the balloon in your left hand with the uninflated end pointing right. Form a 1-inch bubble for the head. To make one side of the antlers, form two 1½-inch bubbles and lock twist them at the base.

2 To make the other side of the antlers, form two 1½-inch bubbles and lock twist them at the base.

3 To make the neck and front legs, form three 2-inch bubbles. Lock twist the last two at the base to complete the front legs.

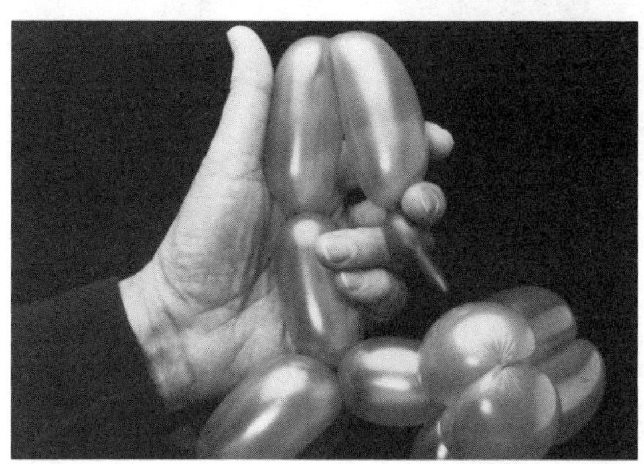

4 Form a 3-inch bubble for the body. To make the back legs, form two 2-inch bubbles and lock twist them at the base. Leave a small bubble of air at the base of the tail to hold the back legs in place and complete the figure.

RAM/BIGHORN SHEEP

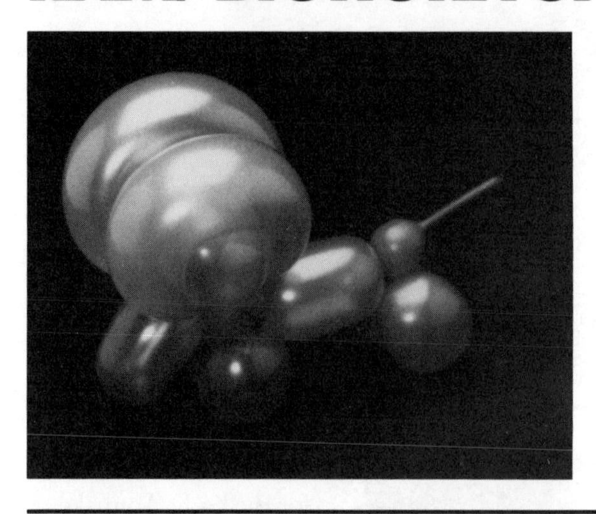

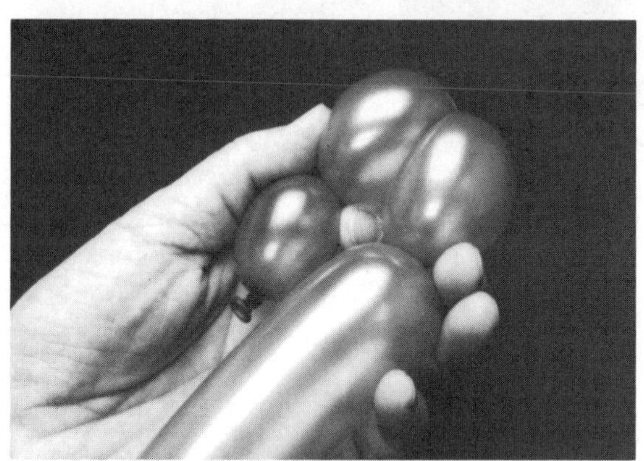

1 Inflate the balloon, leaving a 6-inch uninflated end. Tie a knot. Hold the balloon in your left hand with the uninflated end pointing right. To make the head and one horn, form three 1-inch bubbles and lock twist the last two at the base.

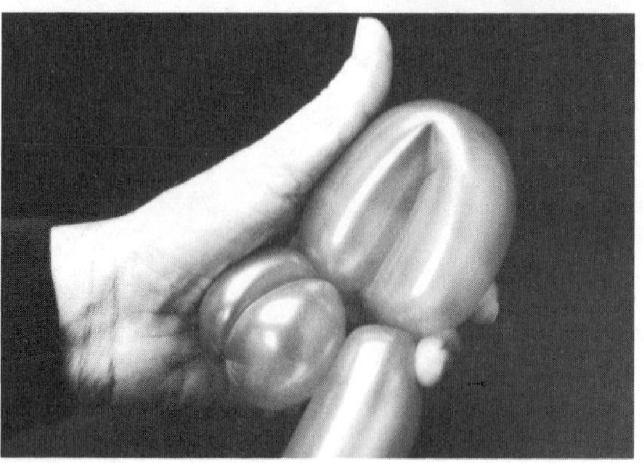

2 Then, form a 1½-inch loop and lock twist the ends.

3 To make the other horn, form another 1½-inch loop and lock twist the ends.

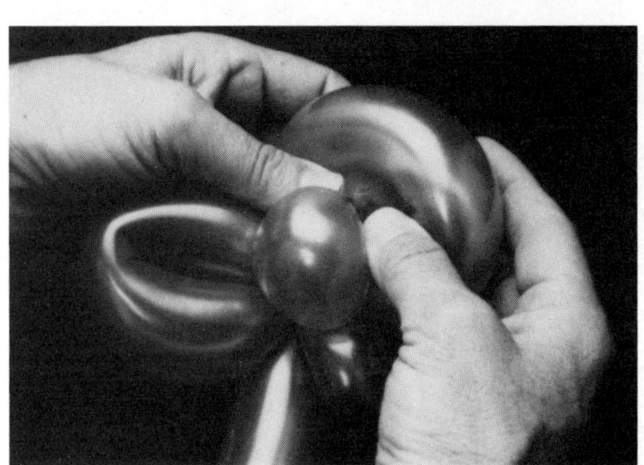

4 Tuck one of the 1-inch bubbles (formed in step one) into the center of one of the loops to complete one horn.

5 To complete the other horn, tuck the other 1-inch bubble into the center of the other loop.

6 To make the neck and front legs, form three 1-inch bubbles and lock twist the last two at the base.

7 Form a 2-inch bubble for the body. To make the back legs, form two 1-inch bubbles and lock twist them at the base. Leave a small bubble of air at the base of the tail to hold the back legs in place and complete the figure.

LOOP AND TUCK

The loop and tuck is used for the head of some animals, the wheels of some vehicles, the tails of some birds, and the head of the doll. It can be formed in two ways: with a small bubble forming the center of the loop and with a long bubble passing through a loop.

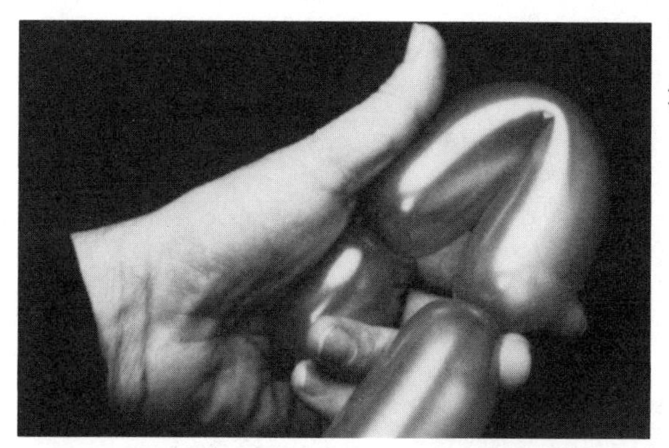

1 For the first version, hold the inflated balloon in your left hand with the uninflated end pointing right. Form a 1-inch bubble, then a 1½-inch loop. Lock twist the ends of the loop at the base.

2 Tuck the 1-inch bubble inside the center of the loop to complete the detail.

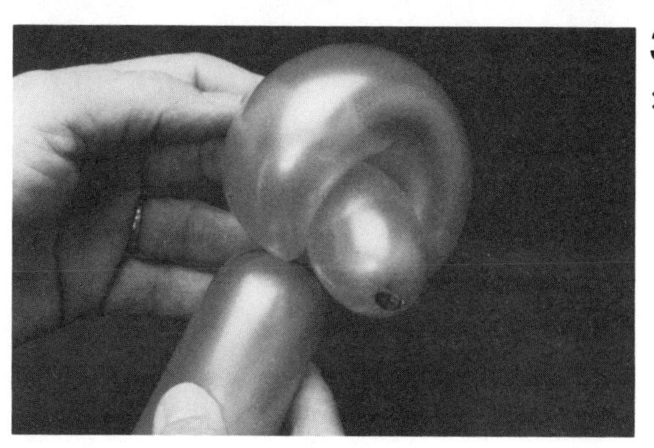

3 For the second version, hold the inflated balloon in your left hand with the uninflated end pointing right. Form a 3-inch bubble and a 1½-inch loop. Lock twist the ends of the loop at the base. Tuck half of the 3-inch bubble through the center of the loop to complete the detail.

FOUR-BUBBLE TWIST

The four-bubble twist is used to add detail to the legs of several figures.

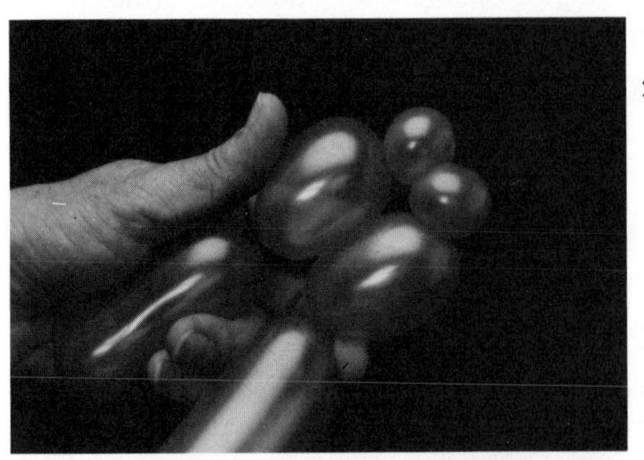

1 Hold the balloon in your left hand with the uninflated end pointing right. Form a chain of a 2-inch bubble, a 1-inch bubble, two ½-inch bubbles, and a 1-inch bubble.

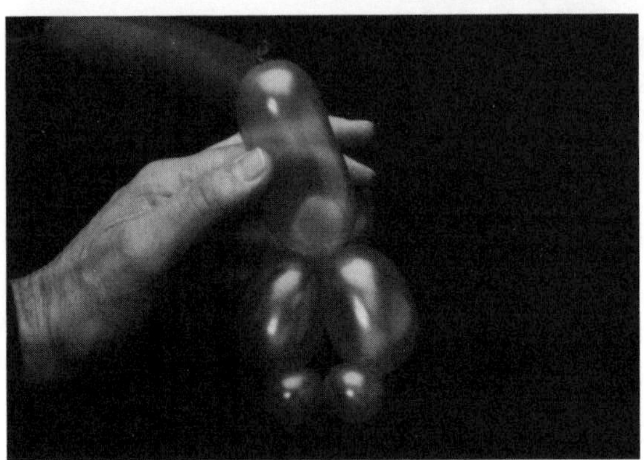

2 Lock twist the two 1-inch bubbles at the base to complete the four bubble leg assembly.

POODLE

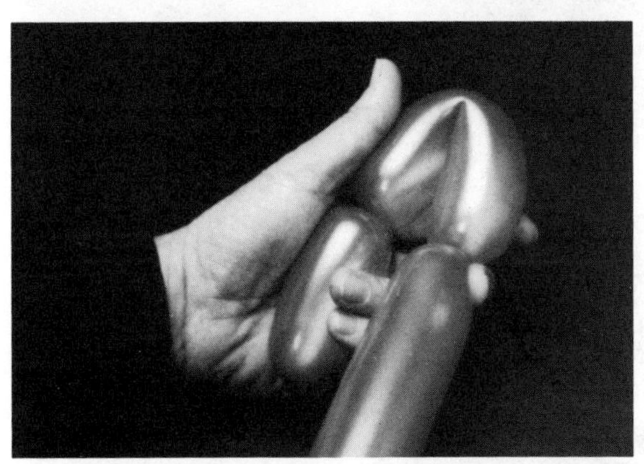

1 Inflate the balloon, leaving an 8-inch uninflated end. Tie a knot. Hold the balloon in your left hand with the uninflated end pointing right. To make the head, form a 3-inch bubble and a 1½-inch loop. Lock twist the ends of the loop.

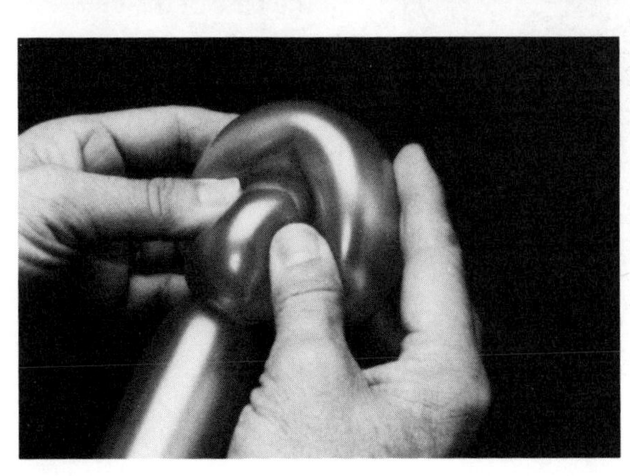

2 Tuck half of the 3-inch bubble through the center of the 1½-inch loop to make the head.

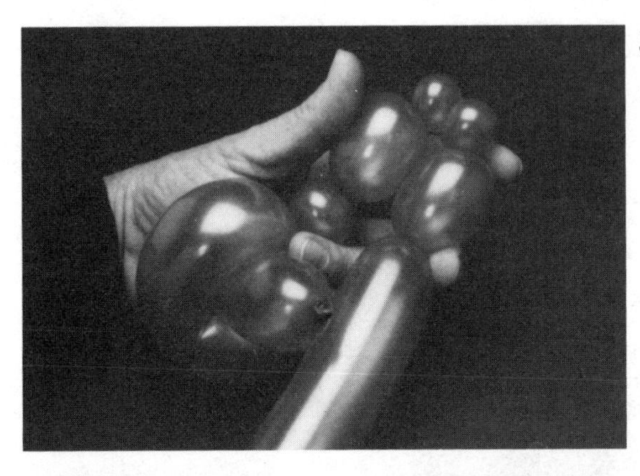

3 Form a 1-inch bubble for the neck. To make the front legs, form a chain of a 1½-inch bubble, two ½-inch bubbles, and a 1½-inch bubble. Then lock twist the two 1½-inch bubbles at the base.

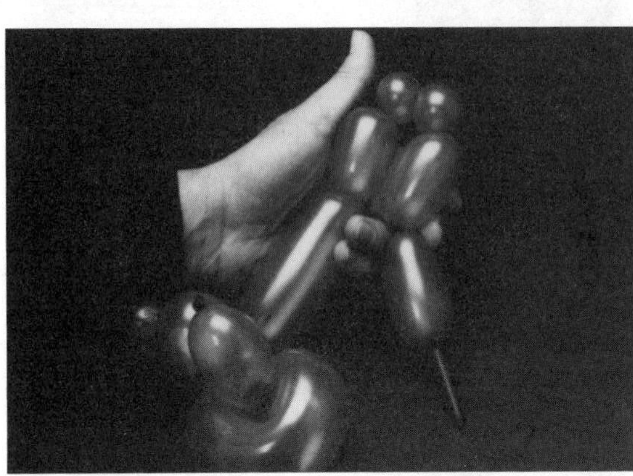

4 Form a 3-inch bubble for the body. To make the back legs, form a chain of a 1½-inch bubble, two ½-inch bubbles, and a 1½-inch bubble. Lock twist the two 1½-inch bubbles at the base.

5 Form a 1-inch bubble at the base of the tail. Squeeze any remaining air into the uninflated tip of the balloon, creating a ball at the end of the tail to complete the figure.

POODLE WITH EARS

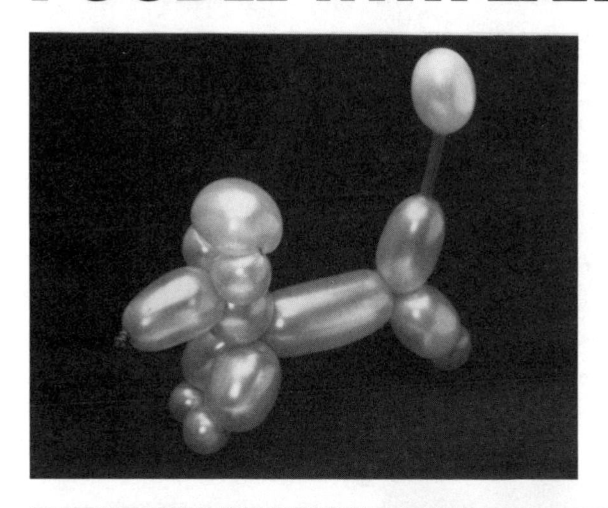

1 Inflate the balloon, leaving an 8-inch uninflated end. Tie a knot. Hold the balloon in your left hand with the uninflated end pointing right. To make the head, form a chain of a 1-inch bubble, a ½-inch bubble, a 1½-inch bubble, and a ½-inch bubble.

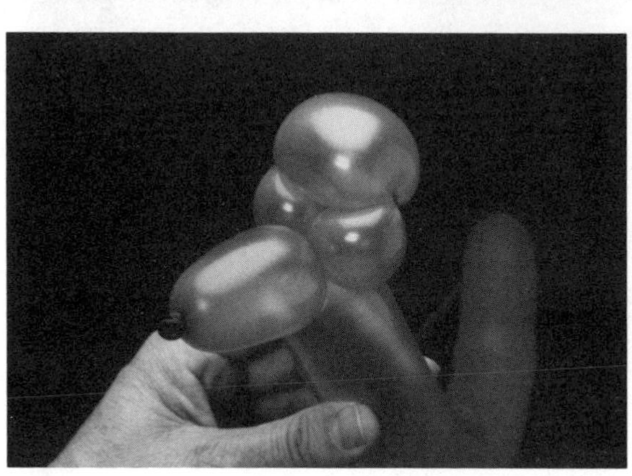

2 Lock twist the two ½-inch bubbles at the base to complete the head.

3 Form a 1-inch bubble for the neck. To make the front legs, form a chain of a 1½-inch bubble, two ½-inch bubbles, and 1½-inch bubble. Lock twist the two 1½-inch bubbles at the base.

4 Form a 3-inch bubble for the body. To make the back legs, form a chain of a 1½-inch bubble, two ½-inch bubbles, and a 1½-inch bubble. Lock twist the two 1½-inch bubbles at the base.

5 Form a 1-inch bubble at the base of the tail. Squeeze any remaining air into the uninflated tip of the balloon to create a ball at the end of the tail and complete the figure.

MONKEY

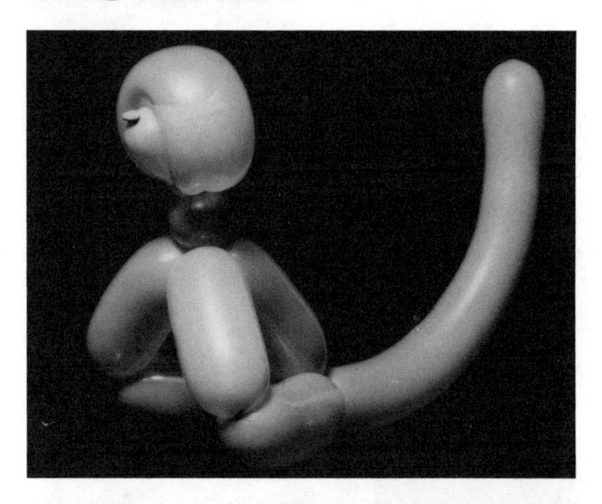

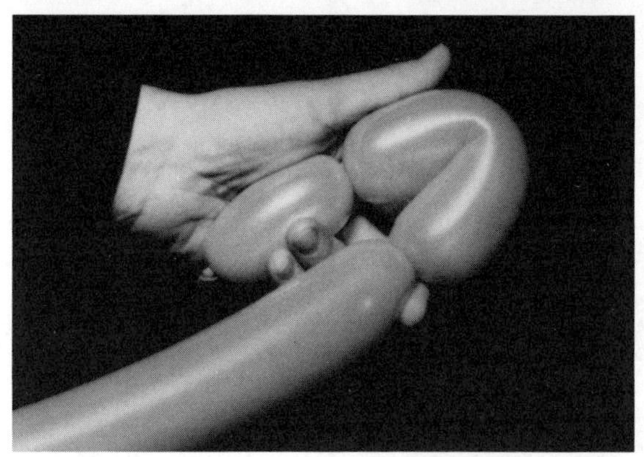

1 Inflate the balloon, leaving a 4-inch uninflated end. Tie a knot. Hold the balloon in your left hand with the uninflated end pointing right. To begin the head, form a 1½-inch bubble and a 2-inch loop.

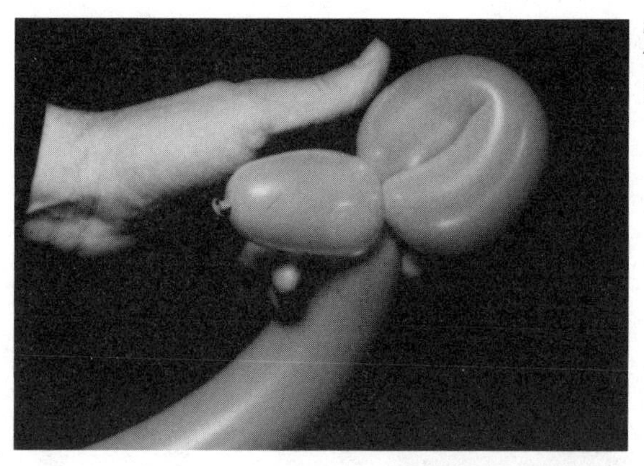

2 Lock twist the ends of the loop.

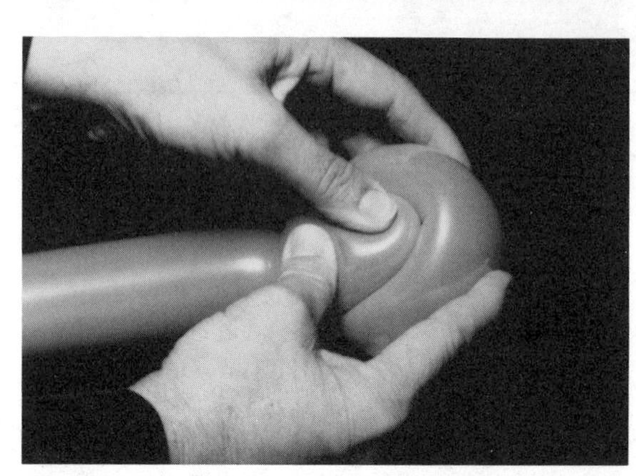

3 To make the face and complete the head, tuck the knot end of the 1½-inch bubble through the 2-inch loop.

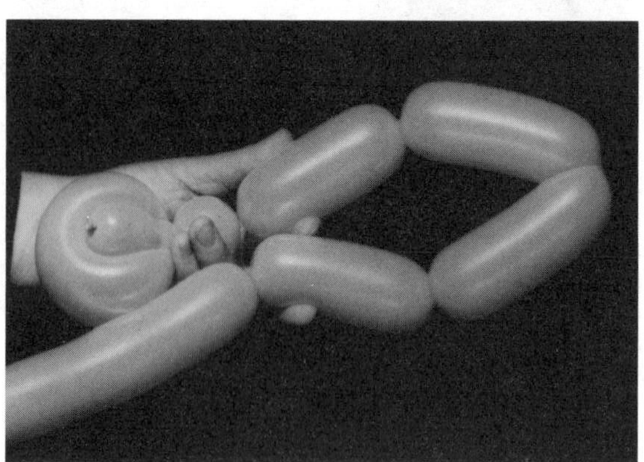

4 Form a 1-inch bubble for the neck. To make the legs, form a chain of a 3-inch bubble, two 4-inch bubbles, and a 3-inch bubble.

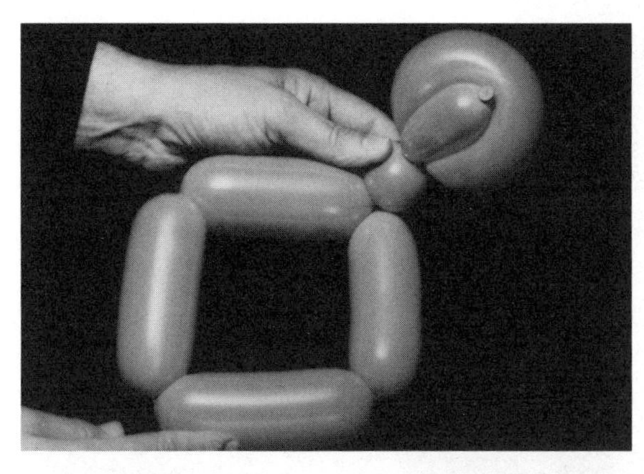

5 Lock twist the two 3-inch bubbles at the base to complete the front legs. The two 4-inch bubbles will form the back legs.

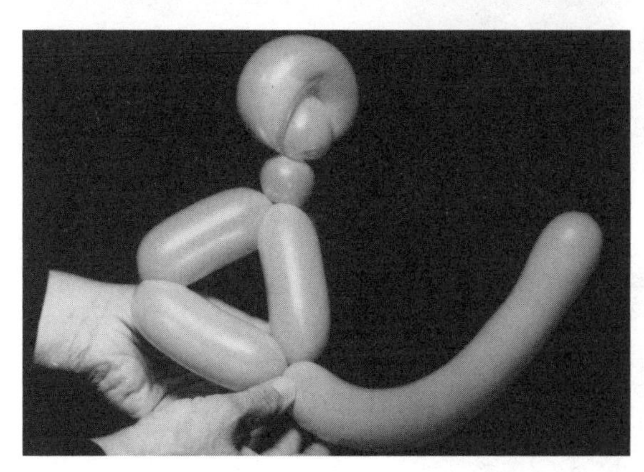

6 Form a 3-inch bubble for the back. Lock twist the base of this bubble with the twist at the base of the back legs. Squeeze any remaining air into the uninflated portion of the balloon to make the tail and complete the figure.

TULIP TWIST

The tulip twist is used to make the tulip and the center of several other flowers, the propeller or jet engine of aircraft, and to add details to such figures as the sword and the pistol.

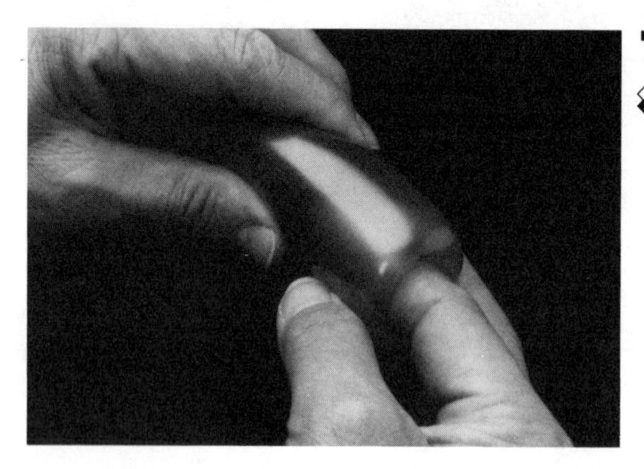

1 Hold the inflated balloon in your left hand with the knot end pointing right and the uninflated end pointing left. With the pointer finger of your right hand, push the knot inside the balloon.

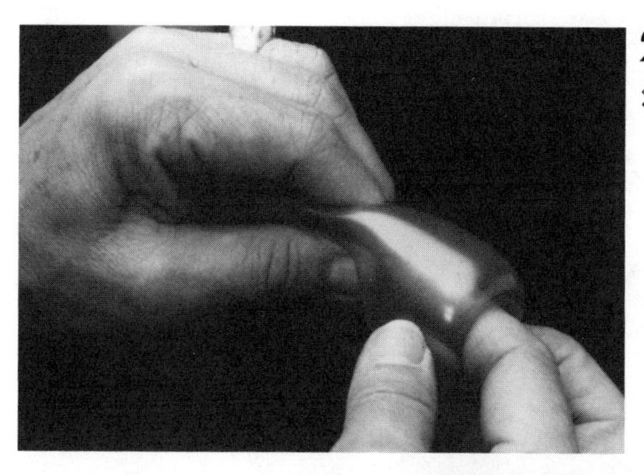

2 With your left hand, pinch the sides of the balloon to grasp the knot inside it. Hold the knot firmly, then carefully slip your right pointer finger from inside the balloon.

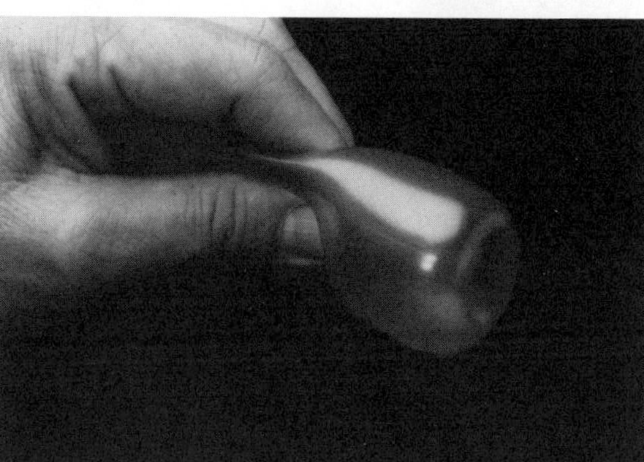

3 With your right hand, twist the balloon three or more times at the base of the bubble where the knot is held. (Be sure the knot is also tucked in the twist.)

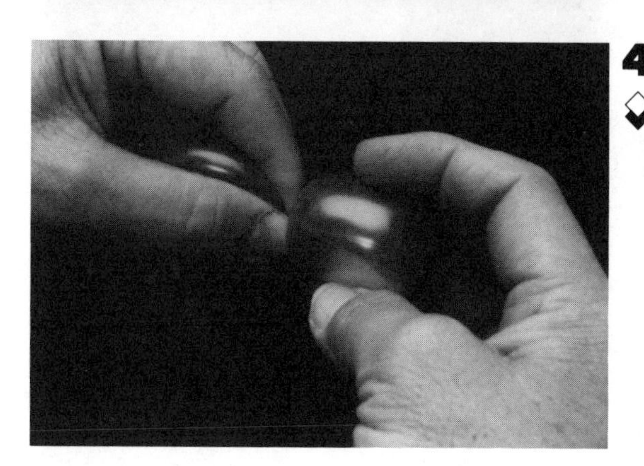

4 To complete the detail, grasp the bubble with your right hand and with your left hand, push the knot slightly into the base of the bubble. Then release the bubble.

TULIP

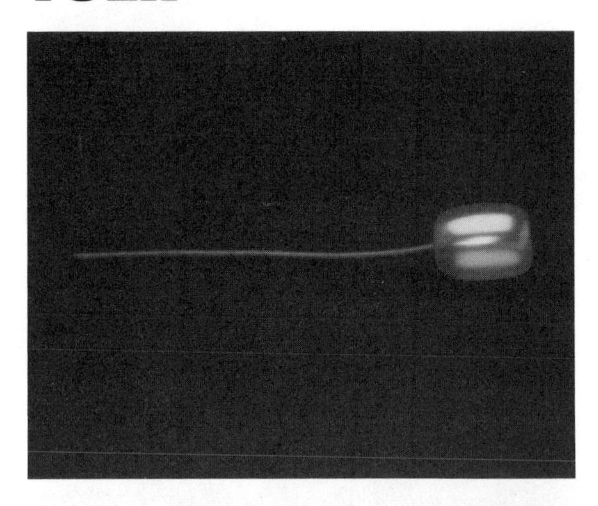

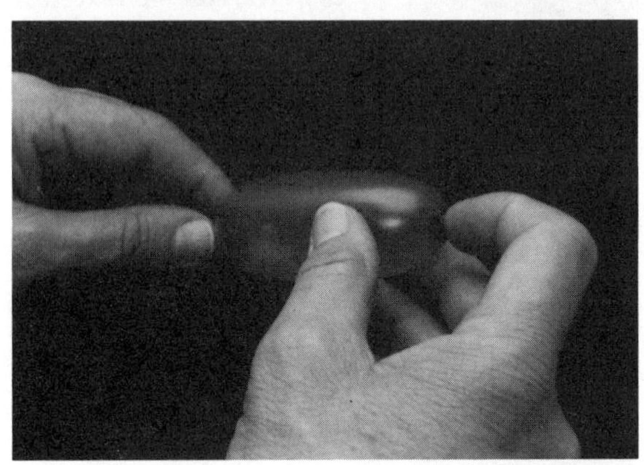

1 Inflate the balloon to form a 2-inch bubble. Tie a knot. With your left hand, hold the uninflated end firmly at the base of the bubble.

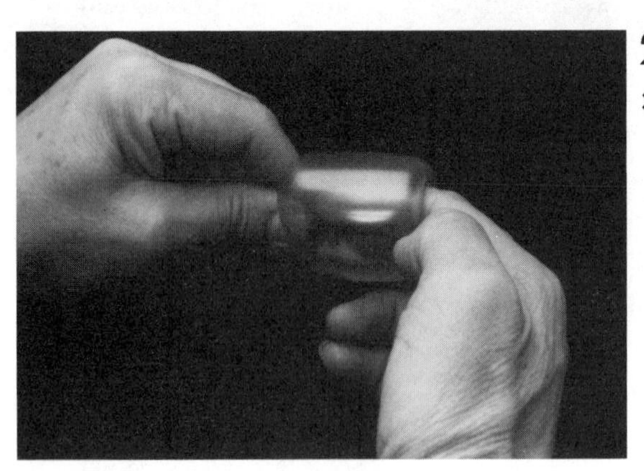

2 With your right pointer finger, push the knot to the base of the bubble and grasp it with your left hand. Do not allow any air to escape from the bubble.

3 While holding the knot with your left hand, use your right hand to twist the bubble three or more times at its base. (Be sure the knot is also locked in the twist.)

4 To complete the tulip, grasp the bubble with your right hand while with your left hand, you push the knot slightly into the base of the bubble. Then release the bubble.

DAISY

1 Inflate the balloon to form a 3-inch bubble. Tie a knot. Hold the bubble in your left hand with the uninflated end pointing right. To begin the center of the tulip, form a ½-inch tulip twist at the knot end. Then form two ½-inch bubbles.

2 To make the petals, hold the tulip twist and the two ½-inch bubbles in your left hand, with the uninflated end of the balloon pointing right. Form a chain of five ¾-inch bubbles.

3 Lock twist the first and last bubbles of this chain to form a loop.

4 Tuck the tulip twist through the five-bubble loop to complete the daisy and the center of the blossom.

ORCHID

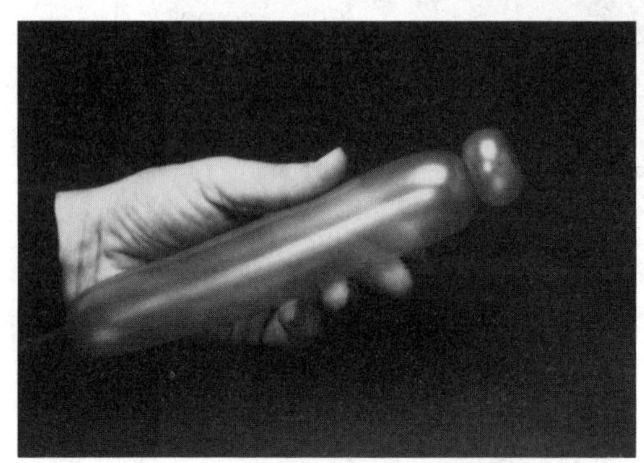

1 Inflate the balloon to form an 8-inch bubble. Tie a knot. Hold the balloon in your left hand with the uninflated end pointing left. Form a 1-inch tulip twist at the knot end of the balloon.

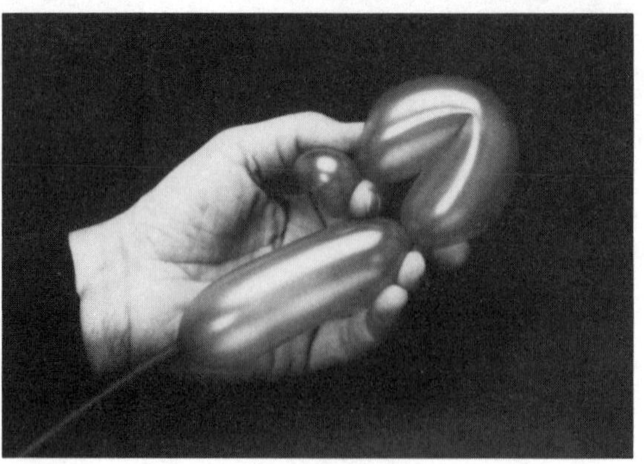

2 Form a 1½-inch loop and lock twist the ends to make the top of the blossom.

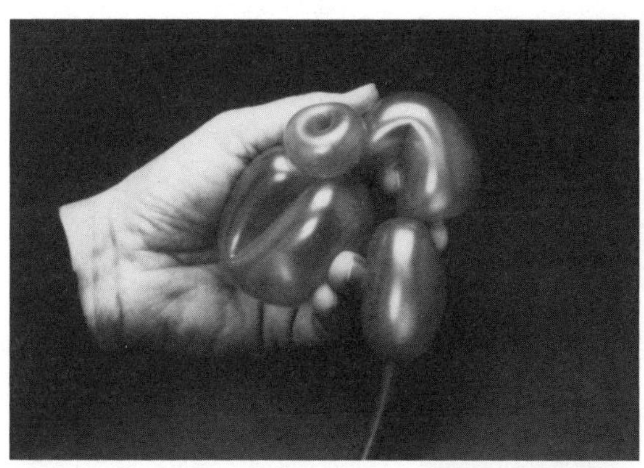

3 Form a 1-inch loop and lock twist the ends to make the bottom of the blossom. The tulip twist should be between the two loops, and the uninflated end of the balloon should point to the rear of the blossom.

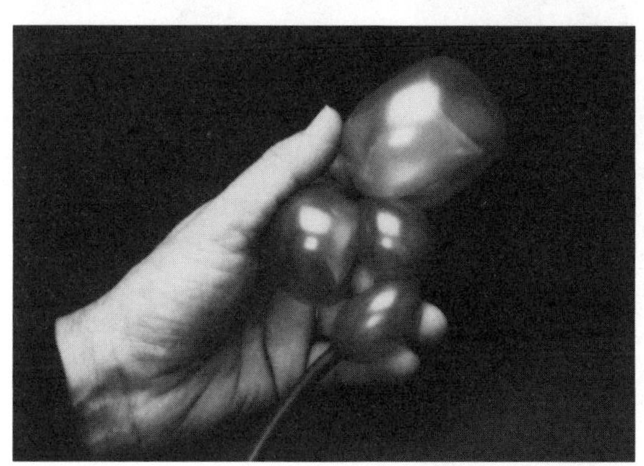

4 Form a 1-inch bubble behind the blossom. Pinch twist this bubble (see page 61) and force the uninflated end of the balloon down to complete the orchid and form the stem.

SUNFLOWER

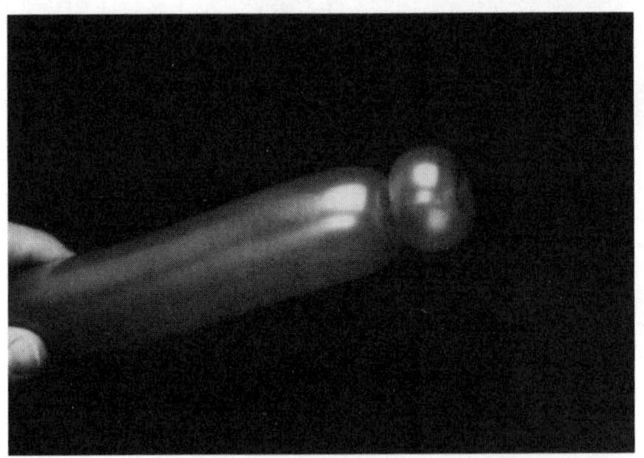

1 Inflate the balloon, leaving a 6-inch uninflated end. Tie a knot. Hold the balloon in your left hand with the uninflated end pointing left. To make the center of the flower, form a 1-inch tulip twist at the knot end.

2 Hold the balloon in your left hand with the uninflated end pointing right. To make the petals, form a 2-inch loop. Lock twist the two ends of the loop at the base of the tulip twist.

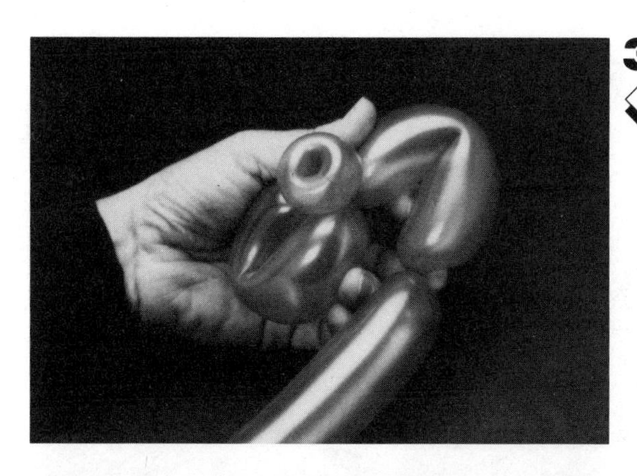

3 Form a second 2-inch loop opposite the first one and lock twist the ends at the base of the tulip twist.

4 Form a third 2-inch loop and lock twist the ends at the base of the tulip twist. Wedge this loop between the other two loops.

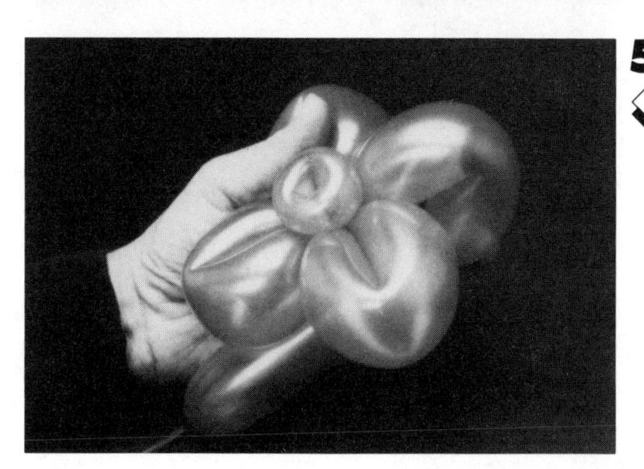

5 To complete the petals, form a fourth 2-inch loop and lock twist the ends at the base of the tulip twist. Wedge this loop between the first and second loops, opposite the third loop.

6 To support the blossom, form a 1-inch bubble behind the blossom.

7 Squeeze the remaining air in the balloon to the base of the uninflated end to shape the stem and complete the sunflower. This leaves a slender section of the balloon between the blossom and the base of the flower, allowing it to sway gracefully.

BOUQUET

A complete bouquet of flowers can be made easily with any of the flowers in this book and a 16-inch round balloon. This bouquet uses one dozen tulips (see page 50).

1 Once about one dozen tulips are made, use an uninflated balloon to tie together the stems.

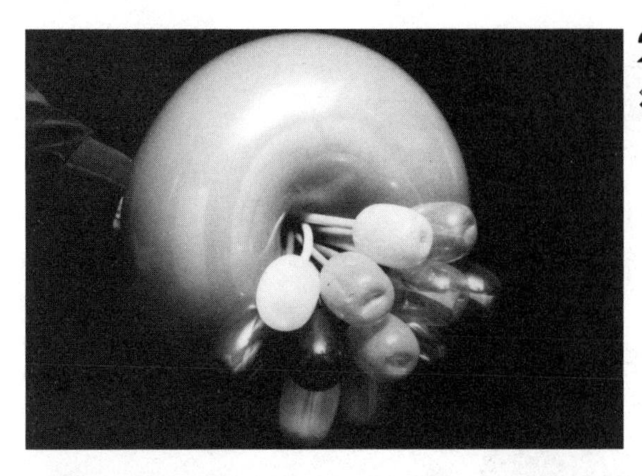

2 Inflate a 16-inch balloon to about 12 inches. Tuck the tied stems into the balloon at the knot, pushing them to the opposite end of the balloon. Squeeze the balloon at that end to grip the stems inside it.

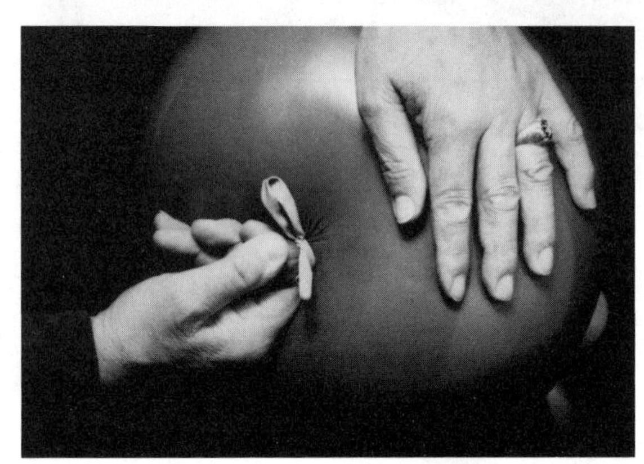

3 Tie another uninflated balloon tightly around the bunch. To complete the bouquet, push the knotted end inside the balloon and out of sight.

PINCH TWIST

The pinch twist is used to make the ears of several animals, to give shape to a series of bubbles, and to hold bubbles in place. Learning to make the pinch twist is the secret to creating more advanced and intricate figures.

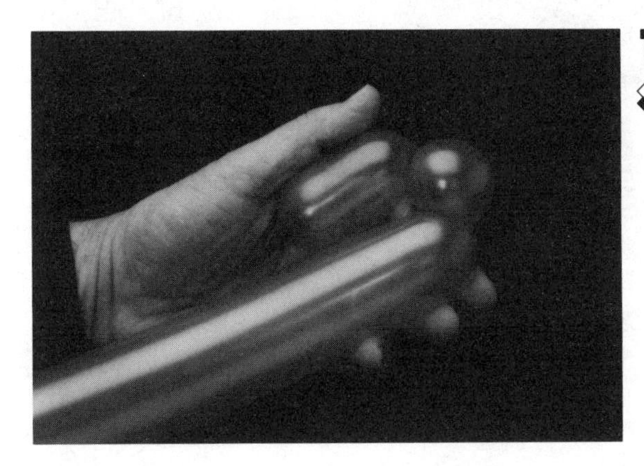

1 Hold the balloon in your left hand with the uninflated end pointing right. Form a 3-inch bubble and a 1-inch bubble.

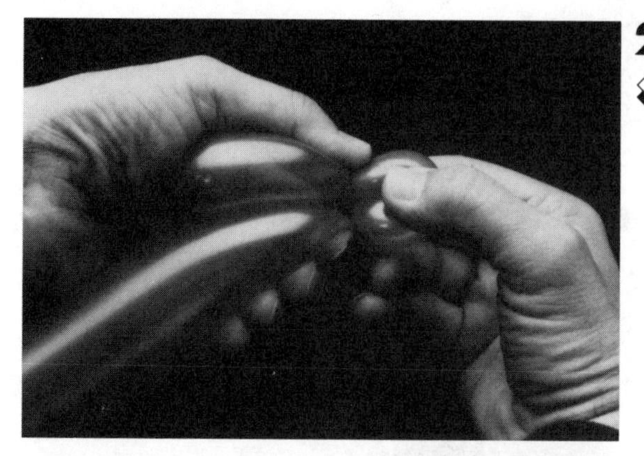

2 Grasp the sides of the 1-inch bubble with your right hand. With your left hand, stretch the bubble out while pinching its ends firmly together.

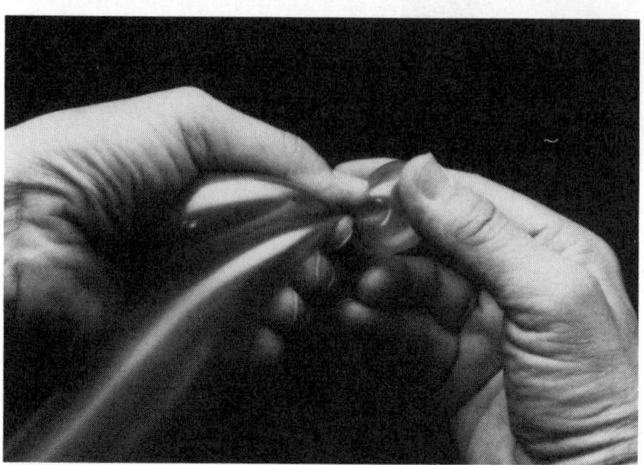

3 To complete the figure, twist the pinched bubble three or more times with the right hand.

HINT: When the pinch twist is done at the knot end of the balloon, pull the knot down alongside the bubble and twist, making sure the knot is also twisted. An end pinch twist is done in designs such as the Horse (page 73, step 2) and the Three-Bladed Helicopter (page 170, step 2).

THREE-BUBBLE SERIES WITH PINCH TWISTS

The three-bubble series with pinch twists is used to make the head and ears of several different animals.

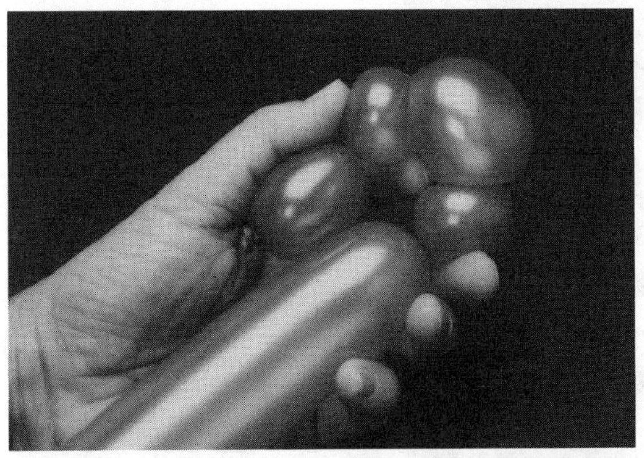

1 Hold the inflated balloon in your left hand with the uninflated end pointing right. To make the head and ears, form a chain of a 1-inch bubble, a ½-inch bubble, a 1-inch bubble, and a ½-inch bubble. Lock twist the two ½-inch bubbles at the base.

2 To complete the head and make the ears, pinch twist the two ½-inch bubbles.

CHIHUAHUA

1 Inflate the balloon to form a 6-inch bubble. Tie a knot. Hold the balloon in your left hand with the uninflated end pointing right. Form a 1-inch bubble for the head. To complete the head, form a chain of a ½-inch bubble, a 1-inch bubble, and a ½-inch bubble. Lock twist the two ½-inch bubbles at the base.

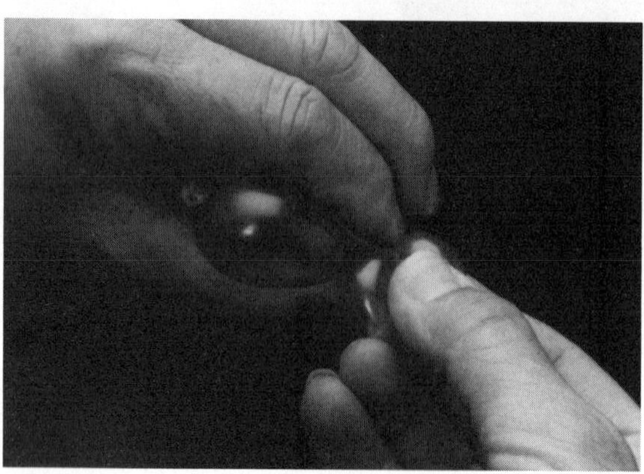

2 To make one ear, pinch twist the first ½-inch bubble.

3 To make the other ear, pinch twist the second ½-inch bubble.

4 Form a 1-inch bubble for the neck. To make the front legs, form two 1-inch bubbles and lock twist them at the base.

5 Form a 2-inch bubble for the body. To make the back legs, form two 1-inch bubbles and lock twist them at the base. Leave a small bubble of air at the base of the tail to hold the back legs in place and complete the figure.

SQUIRREL

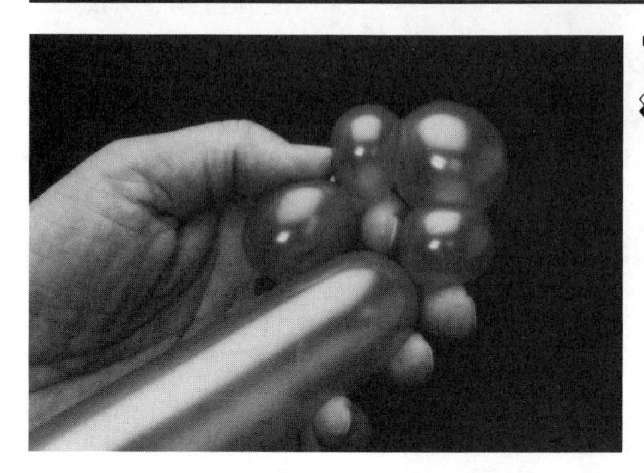

1 Inflate the balloon, leaving a 6-inch uninflated end. Tie a knot. Hold the balloon in your left hand with the uninflated end pointing right. Form a 1-inch bubble for the head. Make a chain of a ½-inch bubble, a 1-inch bubble, and a ½-inch bubble; then lock twist the ½-inch bubbles at the base.

2 To make the ears and complete the head, pinch twist the two ½-inch bubbles.

3 Form a 1-inch bubble for the neck. To make the front legs, form a chain of a 1½-inch bubble, two ½-inch bubbles, and a 1½-inch bubble. Lock twist the 1½-inch bubbles at the base.

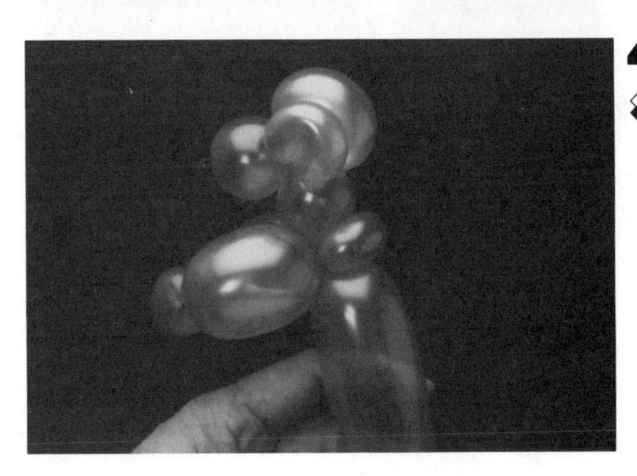

4 To hold the head forward, form a 1-inch bubble and pinch twist it. Position it horizontally where the front legs and neck join.

5 Form a 3-inch bubble for the body. To make one back leg, form a 2-inch loop and lock twist the ends.

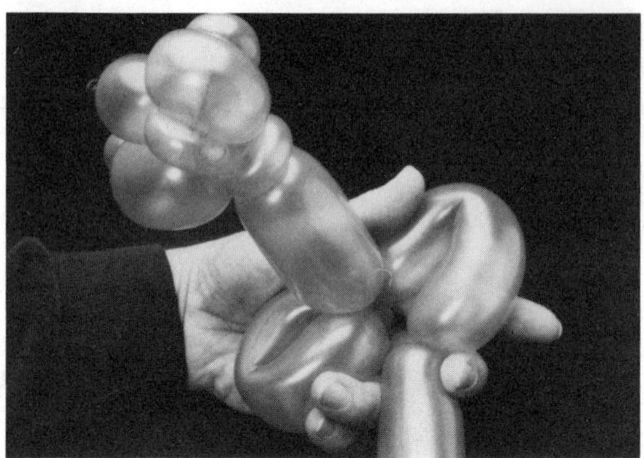

6 To make the other back leg, form a 2-inch loop and lock twist the ends. Curve the tail up behind the body to complete the figure.

KANGAROO

1 Inflate the balloon, leaving a 6-inch uninflated end. Tie a knot. Hold the balloon in your left hand with the uninflated end pointing right. Form a 1-inch bubble for the head. To complete the head, form a chain of a ½-inch bubble, a 1-inch bubble, and a ½-inch bubble. Lock twist the two ½-inch bubbles at the base.

2 To make the ears, pinch twist the two ½-inch bubbles.

3 Form a 1-inch bubble for the neck. To make the front legs, form a chain of a 1½-inch bubble, two ½-inch bubbles, and a 1½-inch bubble. Lock twist the two 1½-inch bubbles at the base.

4 Form a 1-inch bubble at the base of the front legs.

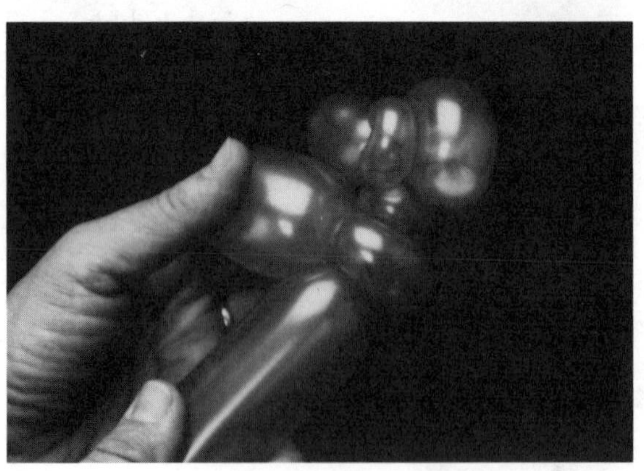

5 To hold the head forward, pinch twist the 1-inch bubble and position it where the front legs join the neck.

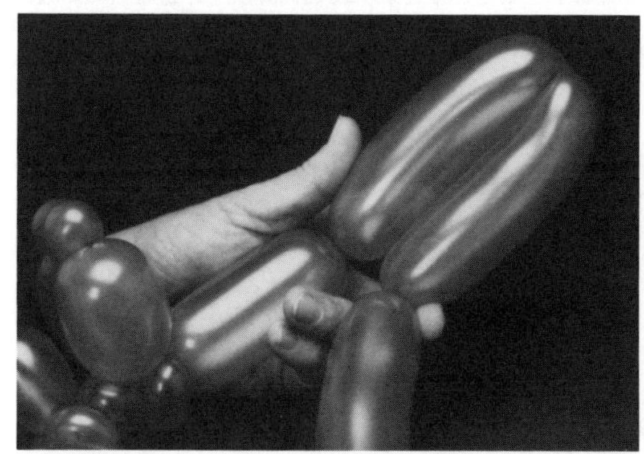

6 Form a 3-inch bubble for the body. To make the back legs, form two 4-inch bubbles and lock twist them at the base.

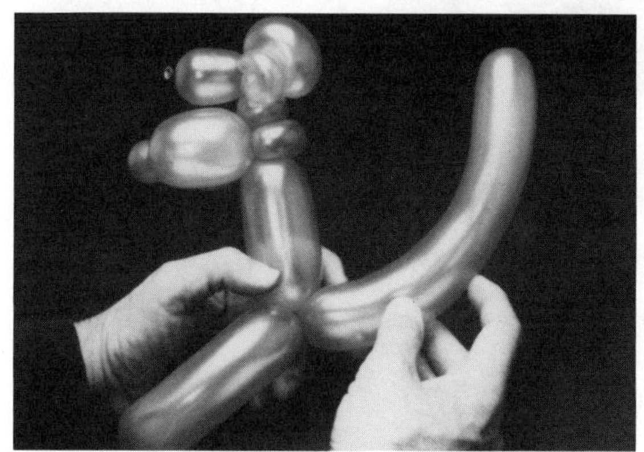

7 Curve the tail slightly upward to complete the figure.

MANE

The mane of a horse or unicorn can be made by adding a chain of small bubbles at the base of the neck and stretching this chain over the ears.

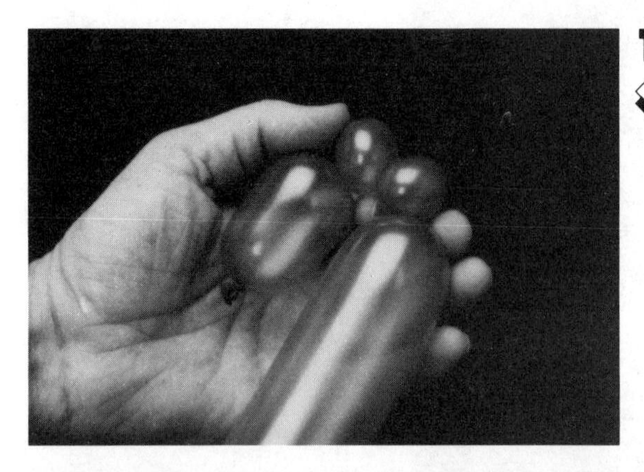

1 Hold the inflated balloon in your left hand with the uninflated end pointing right. Form a 1-inch bubble for the head. To make the ears, form two ½-inch bubbles and lock twist them.

2 Form a 1½-inch bubble for the neck. To make the mane, form a chain of six ½-inch bubbles. Lock twist the first and last bubbles in the chain to form a loop.

3 To complete the mane, stretch this loop over the ears, then wedge the ears between the third and fourth bubbles of the mane.

HORSE

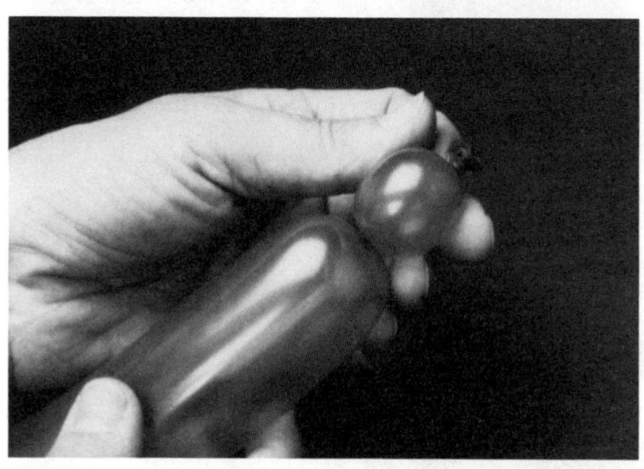

1 Inflate the balloon, leaving an 8-inch uninflated end. Tie a knot. Hold the balloon in your left hand with the uninflated end pointing right. To begin making the head, form a soft 1-inch bubble at the knot end of the balloon.

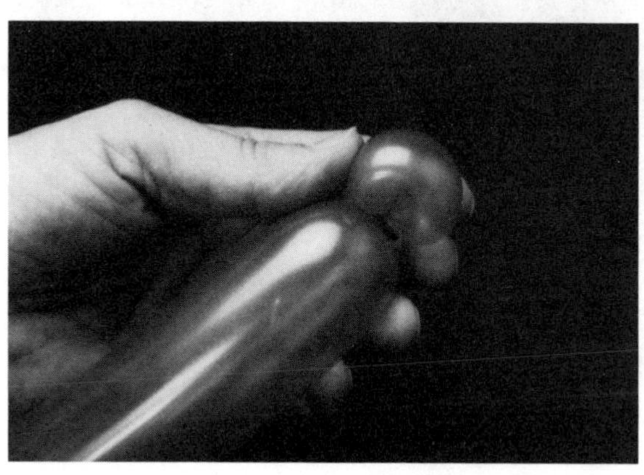

2 Pinch twist the bubble.

3 To make the mouth, twist the bubble in half, twisting each half three or four times.

4 Form a 1-inch bubble for the head. To make the ears, form two ½-inch bubbles and lock twist them at the base.

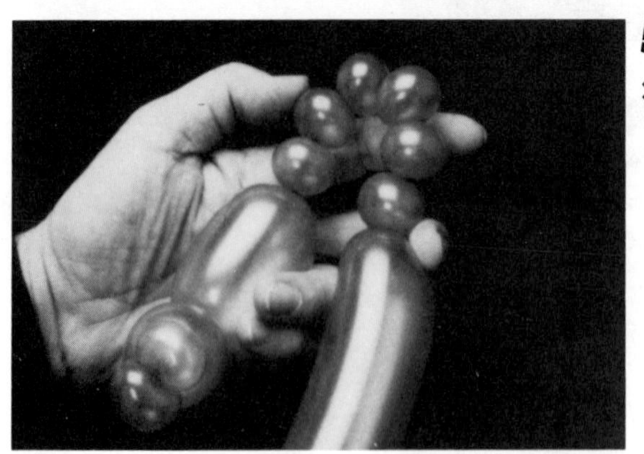

5 Form a 2-inch bubble for the neck. To make the mane, form a chain of six ½-inch bubbles. Lock twist the first and last bubbles in the chain to form a loop.

6 Stretch this loop over the ears, then wedge the ears between the third and fourth bubbles of the chain to complete the mane.

7 To make the front legs, form two 2-inch bubbles and lock twist them at the base.

8 Form a 3-inch bubble for the body. To make the back legs, form two 2-inch bubbles and lock twist them at the base. Leave a small bubble of air at the base of the tail to hold the back legs in place and complete the figure.

ROCKING HORSE

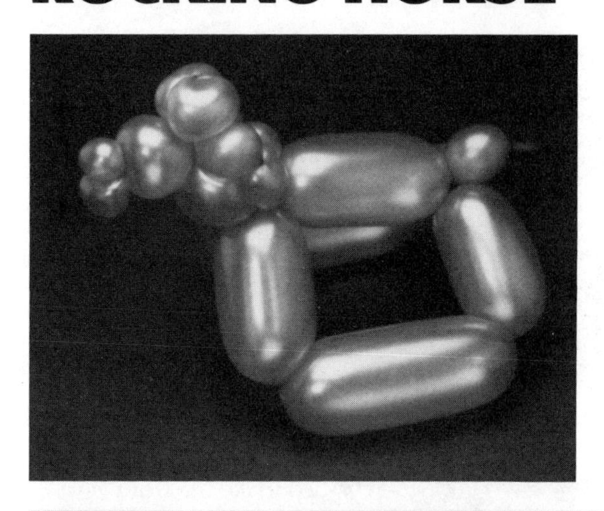

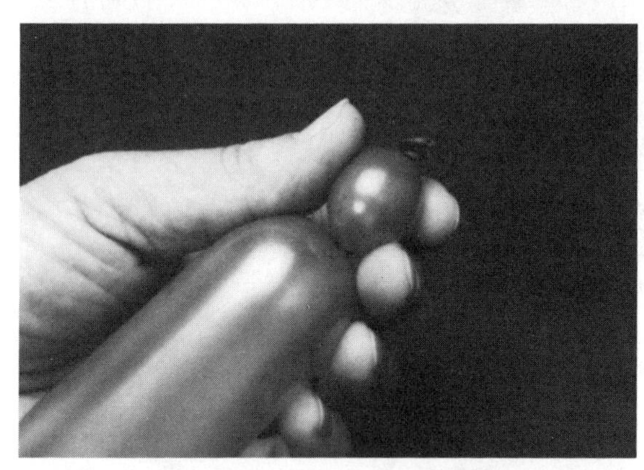

1 Inflate the balloon, leaving an 8-inch uninflated end. Tie a knot. Hold the balloon in your left hand with the uninflated end pointing right. Form a soft 1-inch bubble at the knot end.

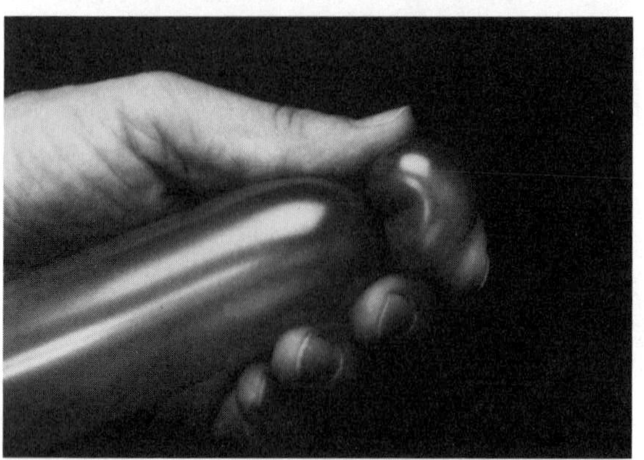

2 Pinch twist the bubble.

3 To make the mouth, twist the bubble in half, twisting each half three or four times.

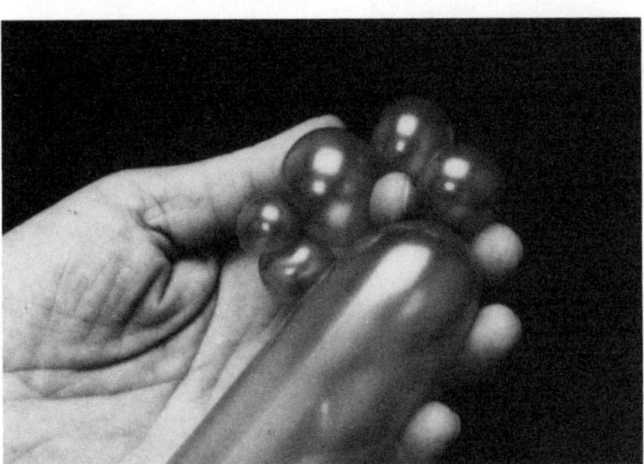

4 Form a ¾-inch bubble for the head. To make the ears, form two ½-inch bubbles and lock twist them at the base.

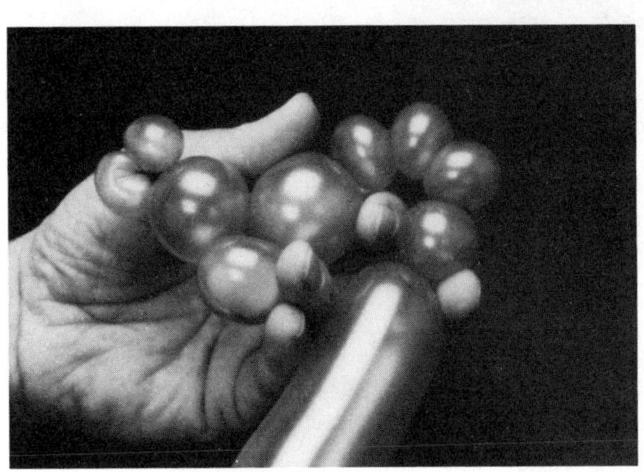

5 Form a 1-inch bubble for the neck. To make the mane, form a chain of four ½-inch bubbles. Lock twist the first and last bubbles in the chain to form a loop.

6 Stretch this loop over the ears, then wedge the ears between the second and third bubbles in the chain to complete the mane.

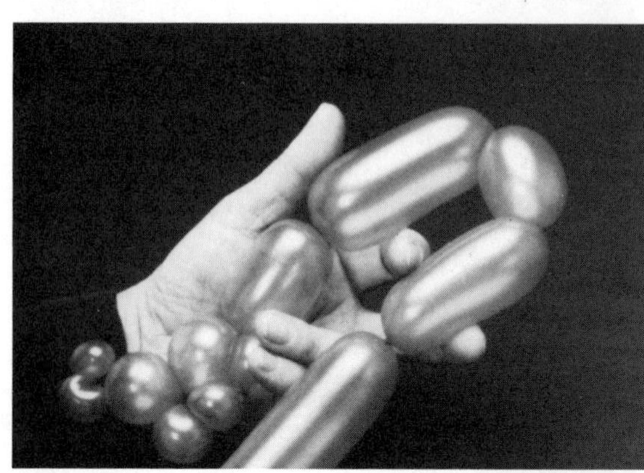

7 To make the body and one of the rockers, form a 2-inch bubble, a 3-inch bubble, and two 2-inch bubbles. Lock twist the first and third 2-inch bubbles at the base.

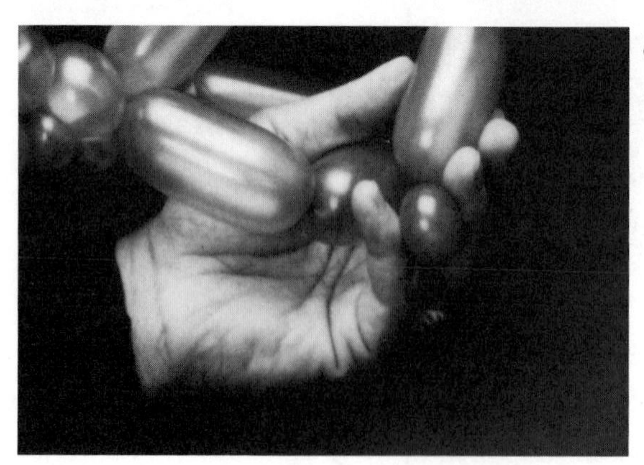

8 To make the other rocker, form a 2-inch bubble, a 3-inch, and a 2-inch bubble. Lock twist the second 2-inch bubble where the back leg joins the body and tail. Leave a small bubble of air at the base of the tail to hold the back legs in place.

LION

The mane of the lion is made by forming the chain of bubbles at the top of the neck instead of the base.

1 Inflate the balloon, leaving an 8-inch uninflated end. Tie a knot. Hold the balloon in your left hand with the uninflated end pointing right. To make the head, form a 1½-inch bubble and two ½-inch bubbles.

2 Hold these three bubbles in your left hand to keep them twisted. Form a chain of five ¾-inch bubbles. Lock twist the first and last bubbles in the chain to form a loop.

3 Tuck the 1½-inch bubble formed in step one through the loop to complete the head and mane.

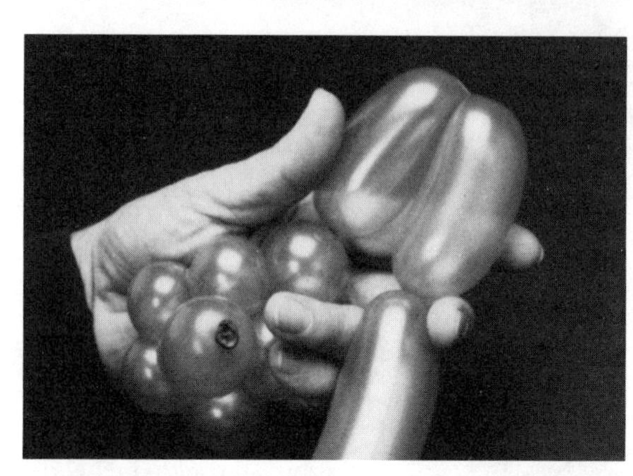

4 Form a 1-inch bubble for the neck. To make the front legs, form two 1½-inch bubbles and lock twist them at the base.

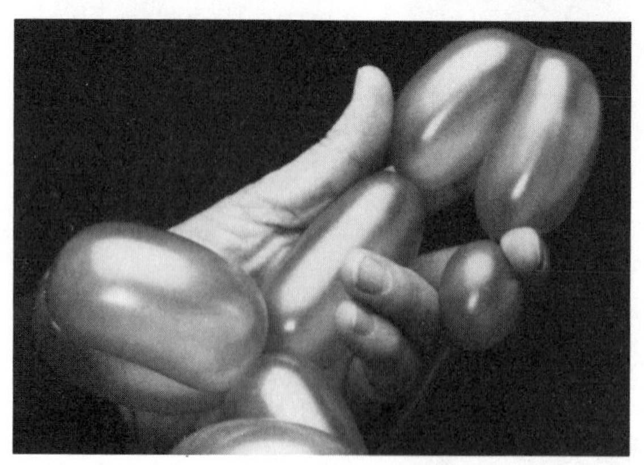

5 Form a 3-inch bubble for the body. To make the back legs, form two 1½-inch bubbles and lock twist them at the base. Leave a small bubble of air at the base of the tail to hold the back legs in place and complete the figure.

LAMB

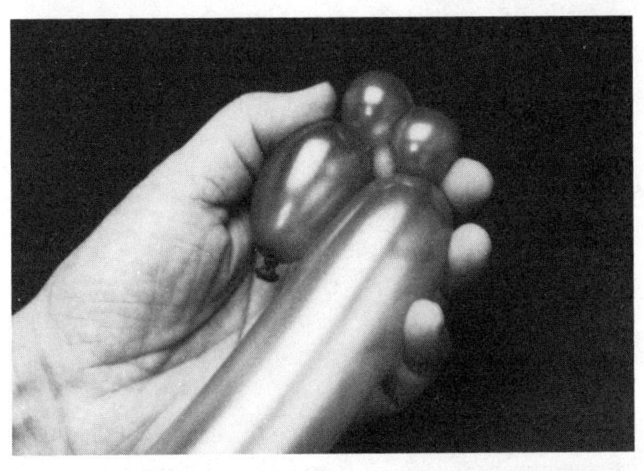

1 Inflate the balloon, leaving an 8-inch uninflated end. Tie a knot. Hold the balloon in your left hand with the uninflated end pointing right. Form a 1-inch bubble to begin the head. To make the ears, form two ½-inch bubbles and lock twist them at the base.

2 Form a chain of seven ½-inch bubbles. Lock twist the third and last bubbles in the chain at the base to make a five-bubble loop.

3 Tuck the head and ears through the loop to complete the head.

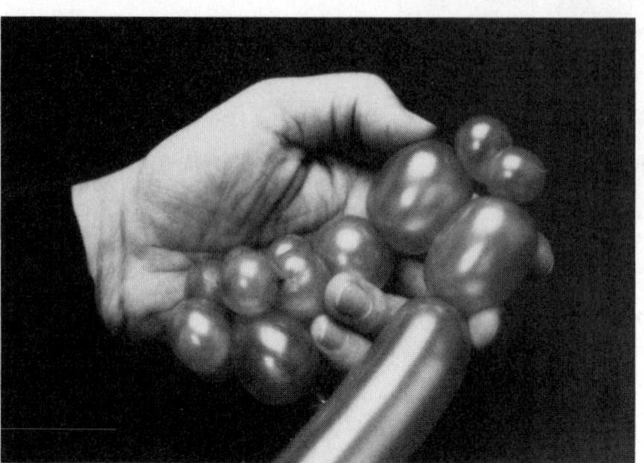

4 Form a 1-inch bubble for the neck. To make the front legs, form a chain of a 1½-inch bubble, two ½-inch bubbles, and a 1½-inch bubble. Lock twist the 1½-inch bubbles at the base.

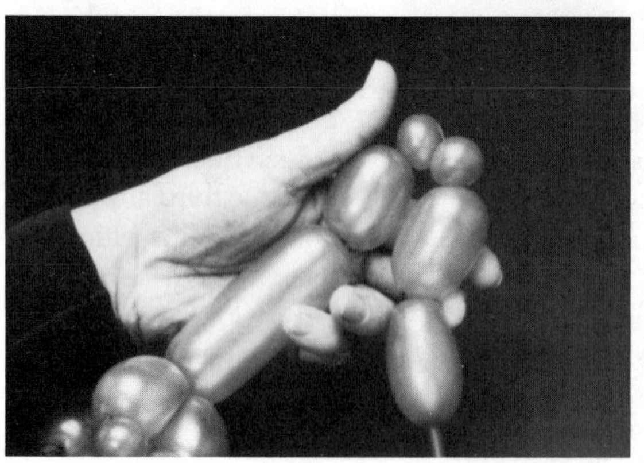

5 Form a 2-inch bubble for the body. To make the back legs, form a chain of a 1½-inch bubble, two ½-inch bubbles, and a 1½-inch bubble. Lock twist the 1½-inch bubbles at the base. Leave a small bubble of air at the base of the tail to hold the back legs in place and complete the figure.

FIVE-BUBBLE SERIES WITH PINCH TWISTS

A five-bubble series with pinch twists is used to make the head of several figures, such as the teddy bear.

1 Hold the inflated balloon in your left hand with the uninflated end pointing right. Squeeze a small amount of air from the knot end to form a soft 3-inch bubble. Then make a five-bubble series with a 1-inch bubble, a ½-inch bubble, a 1½-inch bubble, a ½-inch bubble, and a 1-inch bubble. Lock twist the two 1-inch bubbles at the base.

2 To make the head, form a 2-inch bubble at the knot end of the 3-inch bubble formed in step one.

HINT: Accomplished balloon artists may find it unnecessary to split the 3-inch bubble in completing this figure.

3 Tuck the 2-inch bubble through the center of the loop.

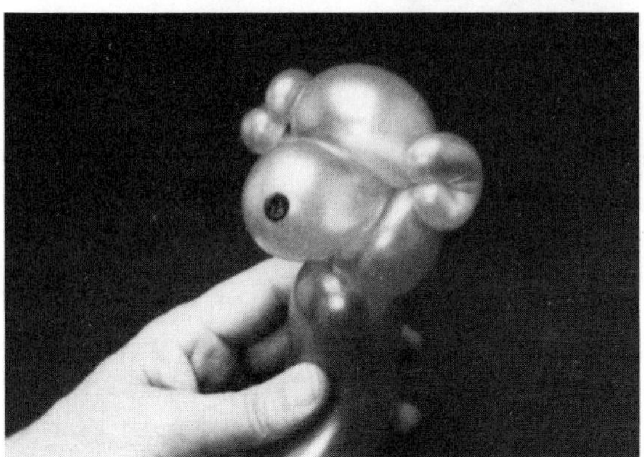

4 Pinch twist the two ½-inch bubbles to make the ears and complete the head.

FIVE-BUBBLE SERIES WITH PINCH AND POP

The five-bubble series with pinch and pop is used to make two details at once, which are later separated by popping the bubble between them. These include arms and legs with feet or paws, handlebars, and the wings and elevators of aircraft. This detail is the only way to create new ends of the balloon.

1 Hold the inflated balloon in your left hand with the uninflated end pointing right. To make a five-bubble loop, form a chain of a 2-inch bubble, a 1-inch bubble, three ½-inch bubbles, and a 1-inch bubble. Lock twist the two 1-inch bubbles at the base.

2 Pinch twist the first and third ½-inch bubbles, twisting each at least four times.

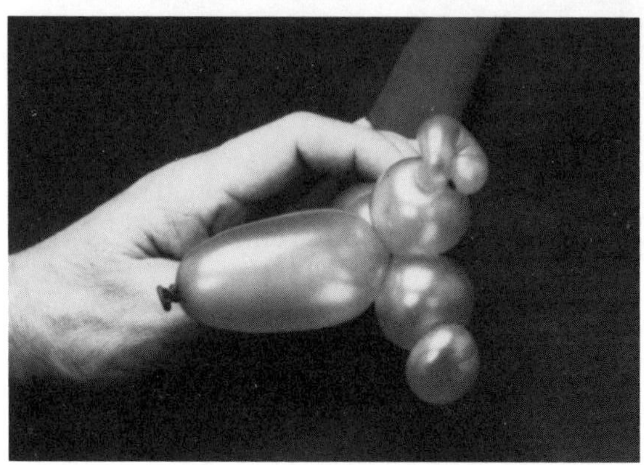

3 Pop the second ½-inch bubble to separate the pinch-twisted bubbles and complete the detail.

TEDDY BEAR

1 Inflate the balloon, leaving a 6-inch uninflated end. Tie a knot. Hold the balloon in your left hand with the uninflated end pointing right. To begin the head, squeeze a small amount of air from the knot end of the balloon and form a soft 3-inch bubble. Form a five-bubble series with a chain of a 1-inch bubble, a ½-inch bubble, a 1½-inch bubble, a ½-inch bubble, and a 1-inch bubble. Lock twist the two 1-inch bubbles at the base.

2 Form a 2-inch bubble at the knot end of the soft 3-inch bubble.

3 Tuck the 2-inch bubble through the center of the five-bubble loop.

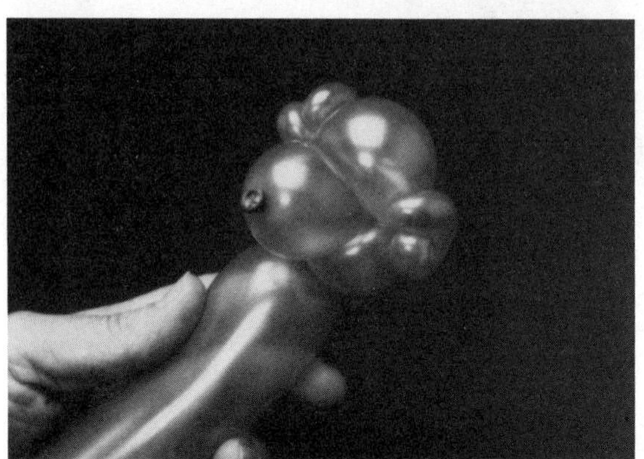

4 Pinch twist the two ½-inch bubbles to make the ears and complete the head.

5 Form a 1-inch bubble for the neck. To make the arms and paws, form a five-bubble pinch and pop series with a 1½-inch bubble, three ½-inch bubbles, and a 1½-inch bubble. Lock twist the two 1½-inch bubbles at the base.

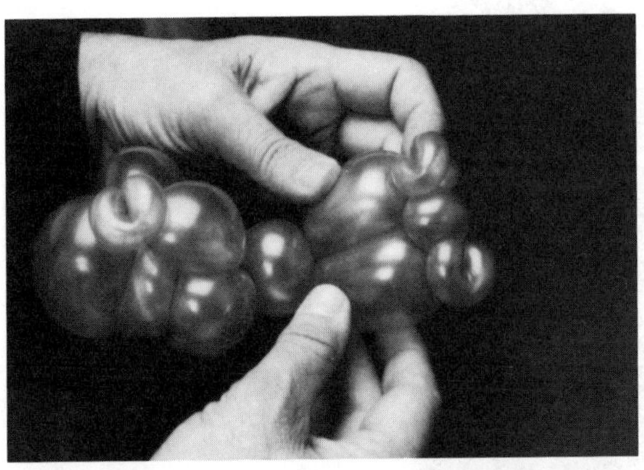

6 To make the paws, pinch twist the first and third ½-inch bubbles, twisting each at least four times. Pop the second ½-inch bubble to separate the arms. (The pinch twist forms the bear's paws.)

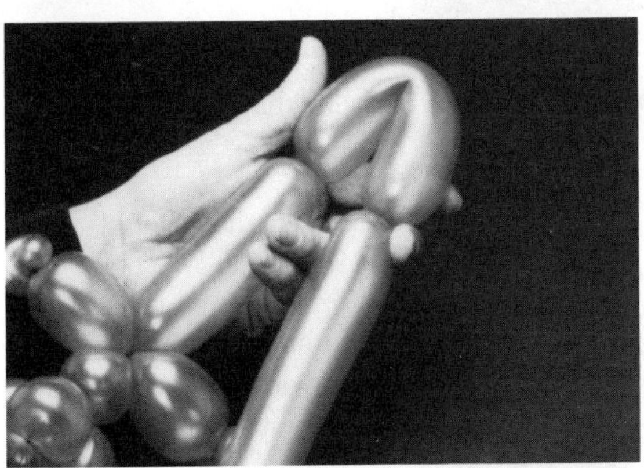

7 Form a 3-inch bubble for the body. To make one of the legs, form a 3-inch loop and lock twist the ends.

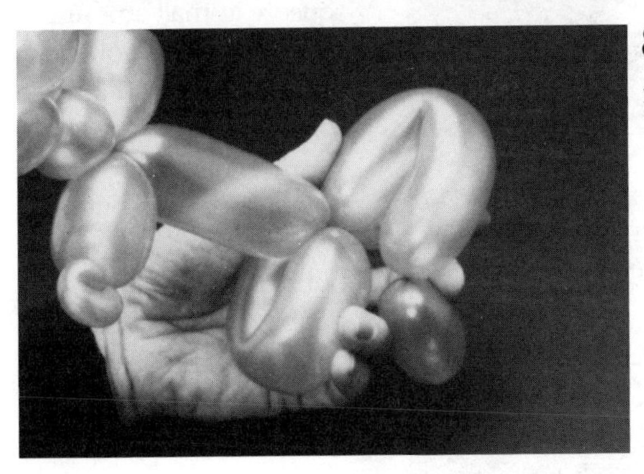

8 To make the other leg, form another 3-inch loop and lock twist the ends. Leave a small bubble of air at the base of the tail to hold the legs in place and complete the figure.

TEDDY BEAR ON A UNICYCLE

HINT: Proportions of this teddy bear design are smaller than those of the standard design to allow for the unicycle.

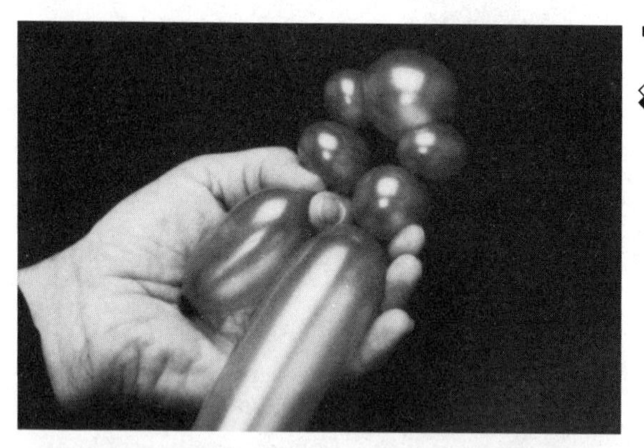

1 Inflate the balloon, leaving an 8-inch uninflated end. Tie a knot. Hold the balloon in your left hand with the uninflated end pointing right. To begin the head, squeeze a small amount of air from the knot end of the balloon and form a soft 2½-inch bubble. Form a chain of a ¾-inch bubble, a ½-inch bubble, a 1-inch bubble, a ½-inch bubble, and a ¾-inch bubble.

2 Lock twist the two ¾-inch bubbles at the base.

3 Form a 1½-inch bubble at the knot end of the soft 2½-inch bubble formed in step one. Tuck the 1½-inch bubble through the center of the loop.

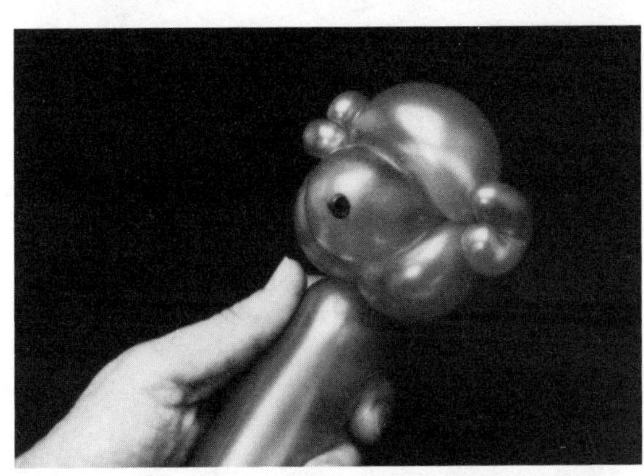

4 Pinch twist the two ½-inch bubbles of the loop to make the ears and complete the head.

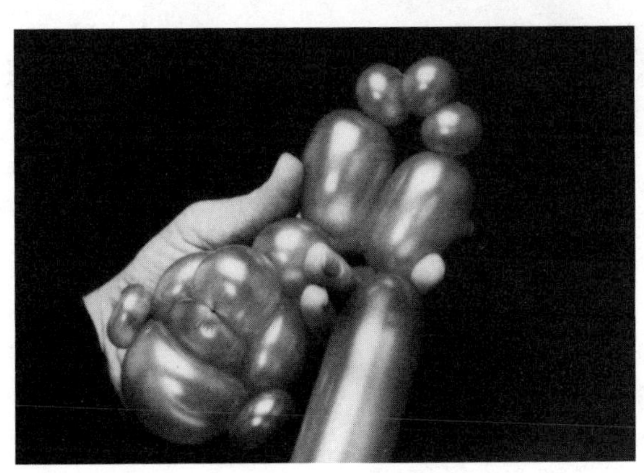

5 Form a ¾-inch bubble for the neck. To make the arms and paws, form a five-bubble series with pinch and pop series with a 1-inch bubble, three ½-inch bubbles, and a 1-inch bubble. Lock twist the two 1-inch bubbles at the base.

6 Pinch twist the first and third ½-inch bubbles, twisting each at least four times. Pop the second ½-inch bubble to separate the arms.

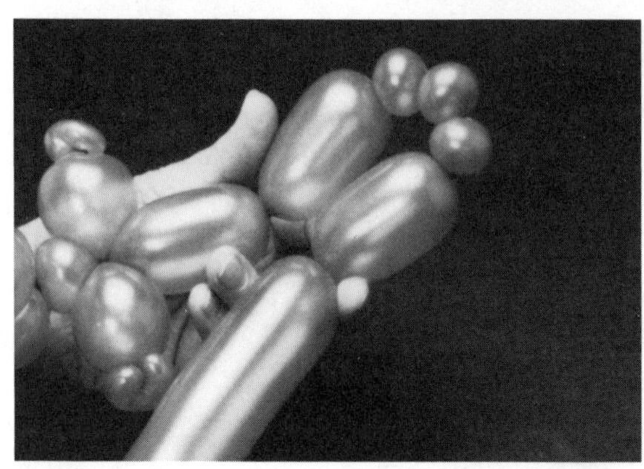

7 Form a 2-inch bubble for the body. To make the legs, form a five-bubble pinch and pop series with a 1½-inch bubble, three ½-inch bubbles, and a 1½-inch bubble. Lock twist the two 1½-inch bubbles at the base.

8 Form a ½-inch bubble at the tip of the remaining part of the balloon. Wrap that part of the balloon around the back legs so one back leg is on each side of the loop. Lock twist the ½-inch bubble where the back legs and the body join to complete the figure.

THREE-BUBBLE ROLL THROUGH

The three-bubble roll through is used for the body of several figures, such as the birds and the turtle.

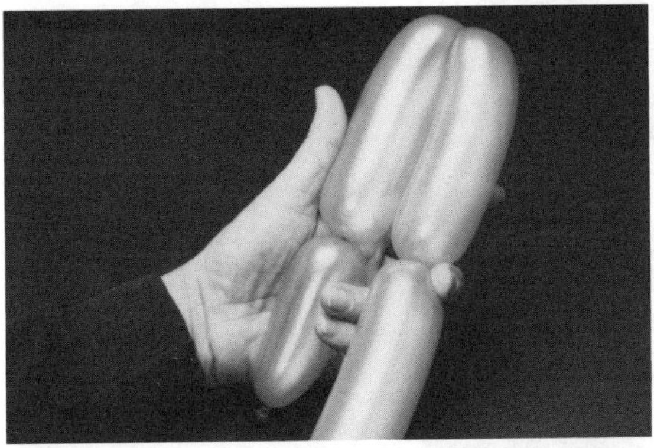

1 Hold the inflated balloon in your left hand with the uninflated end pointing right. Form an initial bubble. Then form two bubbles of equal length and lock twist them at the base.

2 Form a third bubble the same length as the first two and hold it alongside the two-bubble lock twist formed in the previous step.

3 Roll the lock-twisted bubbles completely over the third bubble while pushing the third bubble between them.

LOVE BIRDS

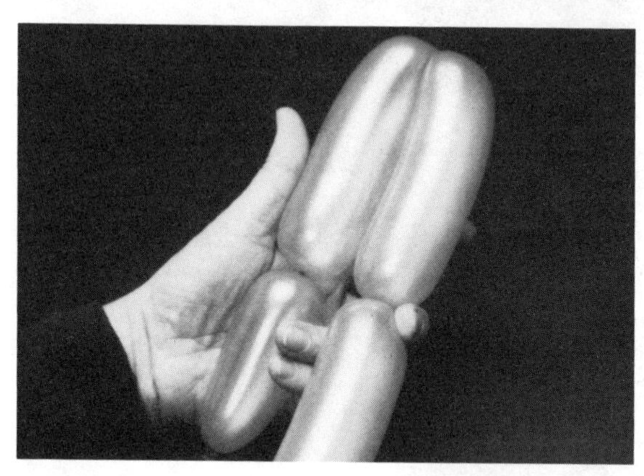

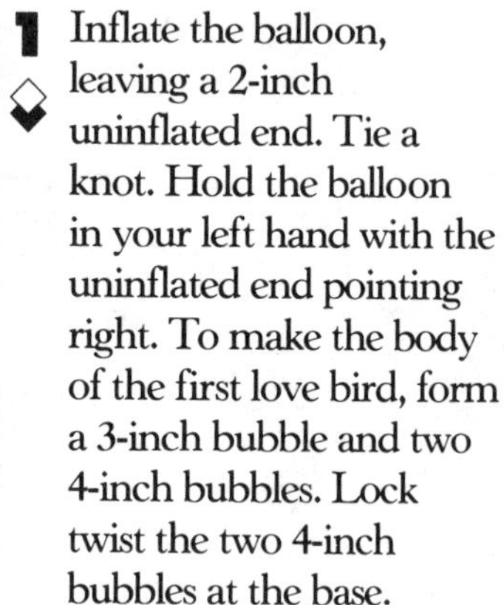

1 Inflate the balloon, leaving a 2-inch uninflated end. Tie a knot. Hold the balloon in your left hand with the uninflated end pointing right. To make the body of the first love bird, form a 3-inch bubble and two 4-inch bubbles. Lock twist the two 4-inch bubbles at the base.

2 Form another 4-inch bubble and hold it alongside the two-bubble lock twist formed in the previous step.

3 Roll the two 4-inch bubbles over the single 4-inch bubble, while pushing the single 4-inch bubble between them to complete the body of the first love bird.

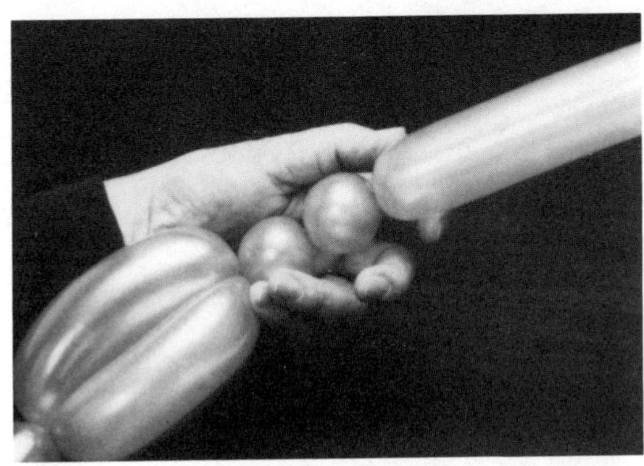

4 Form two 1-inch bubbles to make the heads of the two love birds.

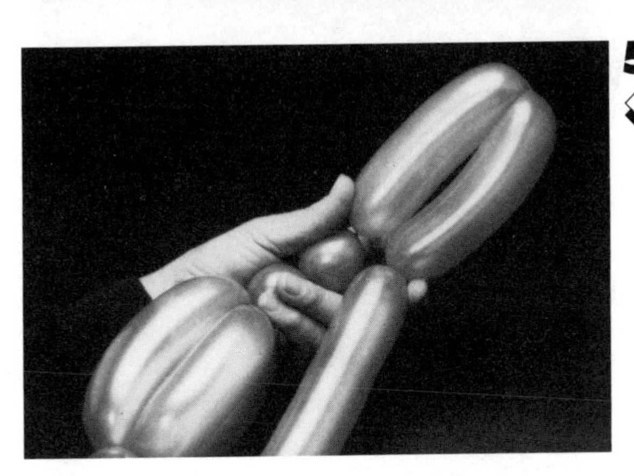

5 To make the body of the second love bird, form two 4-inch bubbles and lock twist them at the base.

6 ◇ Form a 4-inch bubble and hold it alongside the two-bubble lock twist formed in the previous step.

7 ◇ Roll the two 4-inch bubbles over the single 4-inch bubble, while pushing the single bubble between them to complete the body of the second love bird.

8 ◇ To make the tails and complete the figure, lock twist the 3-inch bubble formed in step one and the remaining part of the balloon at the base of the bodies.

LOVE BIRDS IN A SWING

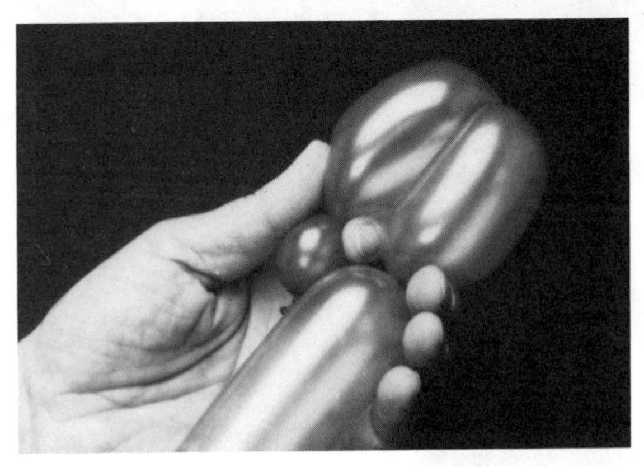

1 Inflate the balloon all the way. Allow a fairly large amount of air to escape to soften the balloon. Tie a knot. To make the body of the first love bird, form a ½-inch bubble and two 1½-inch bubbles, then lock twist the two 1½-inch bubbles at the base.

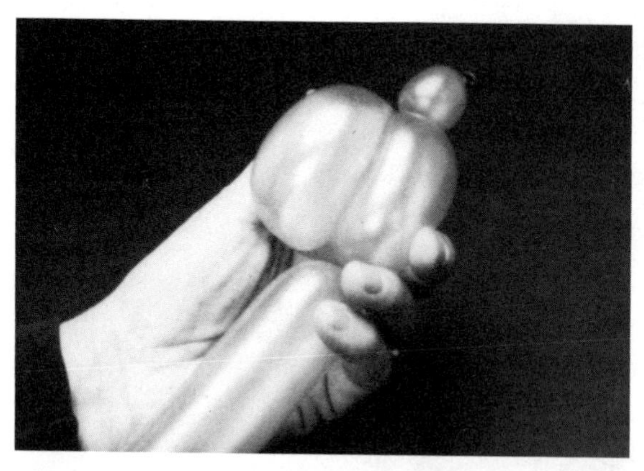

2 Form a 1½-inch bubble and hold it alongside the two-bubble lock twist formed in the previous step.

3 Roll the two 1½-inch bubbles over the single 1½-inch bubble while pushing the single bubble between them to complete the body of the first love bird.

4 Form two ¾-inch bubbles to make the heads of the two love birds.

5 To make the body of the second love bird, form two 1½-inch bubbles and lock twist them at the base.

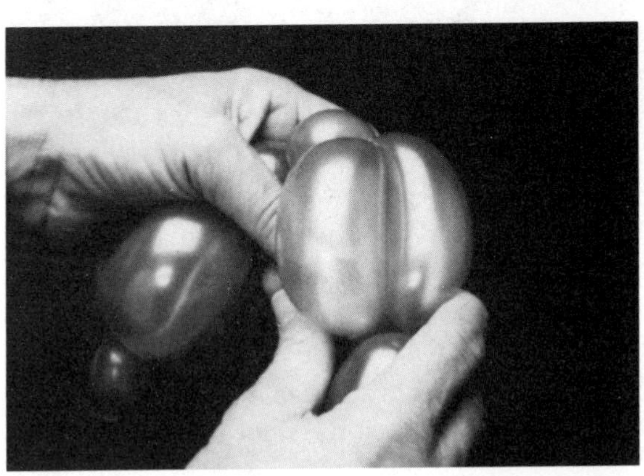

6 Form a 1½-inch bubble and hold it alongside the two-bubble lock twist formed in the previous step.

7 Roll the two 1½-inch bubbles over the single 1½-inch bubble while pushing the single 1½-inch bubble between them to complete the body of the second love bird.

8 Lock twist the ½-inch bubble formed in step one and the rest of the balloon to hold the base of the two love birds together.

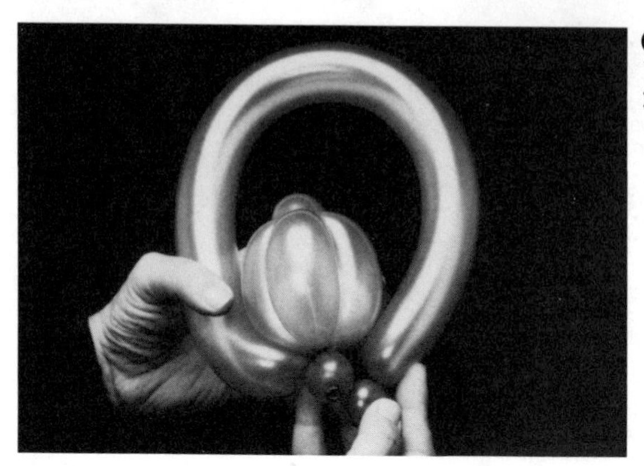

9 Form a ½-inch bubble at the end of the remaining balloon. Form a loop around the two love birds with the rest of the balloon, so that one bird is on each side of the loop. Lock twist the two ½-inch bubbles to make the tails and complete the figure.

PARROT IN A SWING

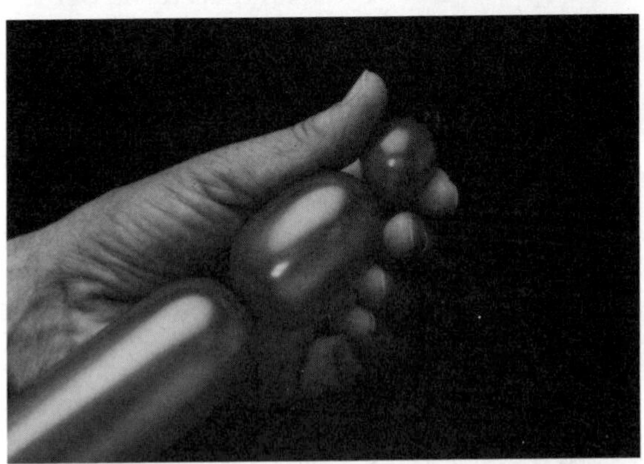

1 Inflate the balloon, leaving a ½-inch uninflated end. Tie a knot. Hold the balloon in your left hand with the uninflated end pointing right. To begin the head, form a ½-inch bubble and a 1½-inch bubble.

2 Grasp the knot end of the balloon with your right hand and stretch it over the 1½-inch bubble. With your right hand, hold the knot and the twist at the base of the 1½-inch bubble.

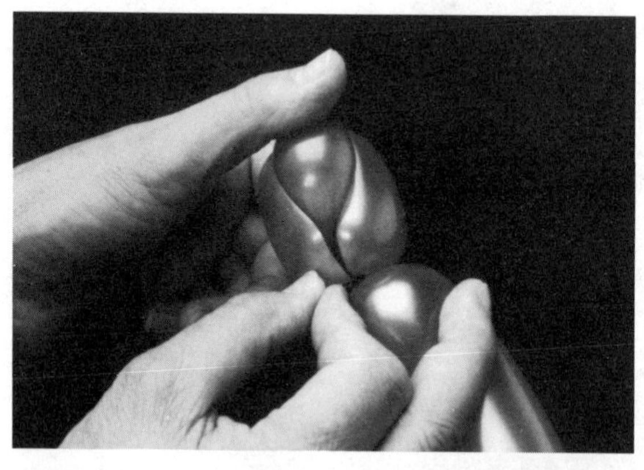

3 Lock twist the knot and the base of the 1½-inch bubble by twisting the two bubbles several times to complete the head.

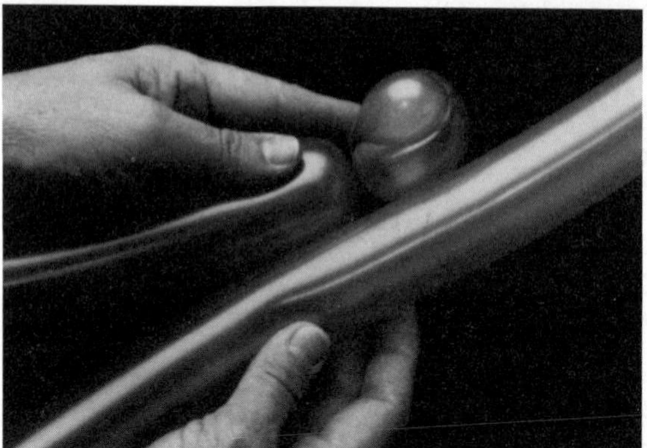

4 To begin the body, bring the uninflated end of the balloon alongside the head so it extends about 6 inches above it. Lock twist the end of the balloon and the head at the base of the head.

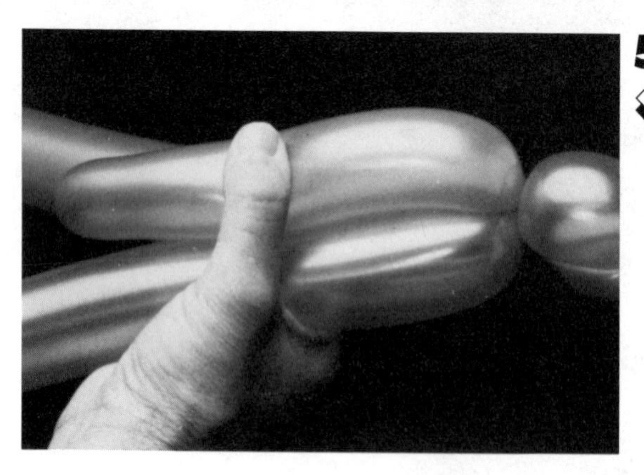

5 Bring together the end of the balloon and the two sides of the loop and hold them with your right hand.

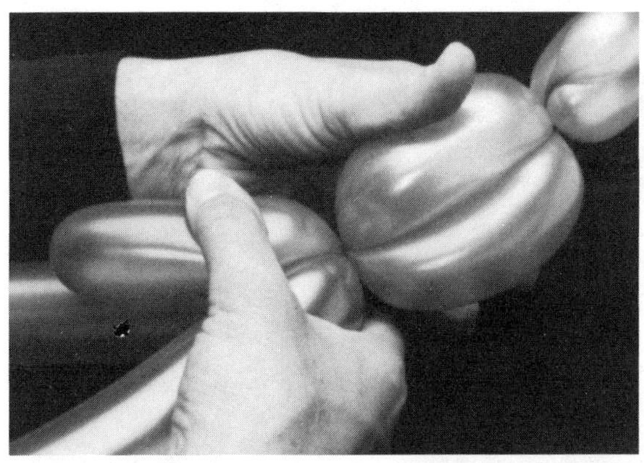

6 Lock twist these three sections together at the middle of the end section to complete the body and make the tail.

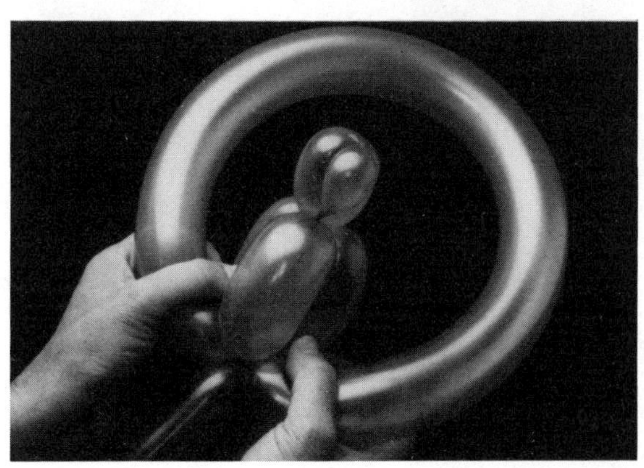

7 To complete the figure and hold the body inside the loop, wedge the body between the two ends of the loop, leaving the tail hanging down.

DOVE

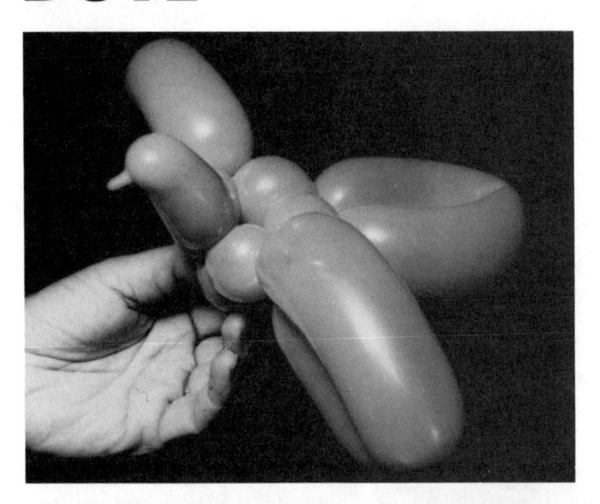

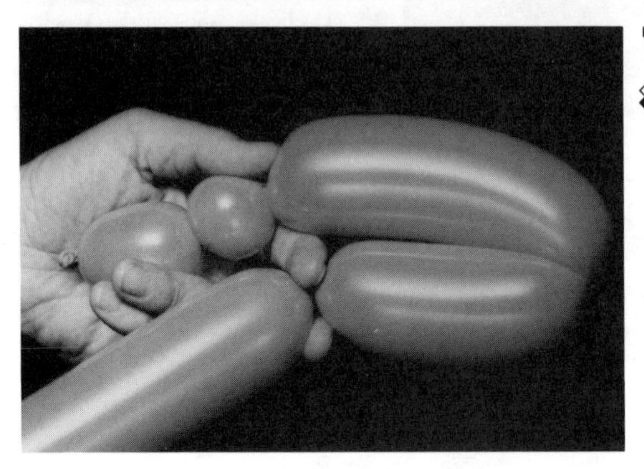

1 Inflate the balloon, leaving a 4-inch uninflated end. Tie a knot. Hold the inflated balloon in your left hand with the uninflated end pointing right. To make one wing, form a chain of a 1½-inch bubble, a 1-inch bubble, a 4-inch bubble, and a 3-inch bubble.

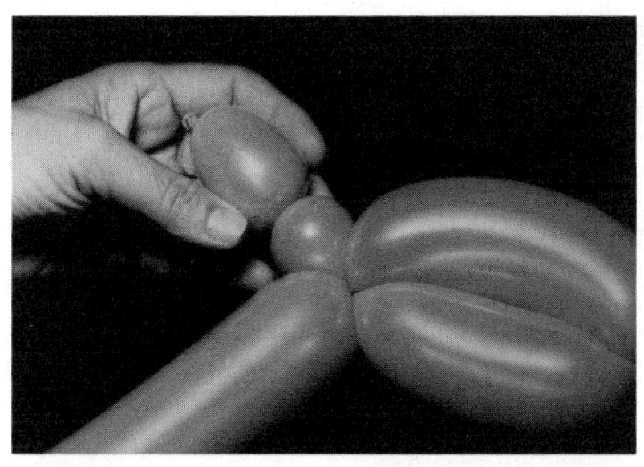

2 Lock twist the 4-inch bubble and the 3-inch bubble at the base, twisting them opposite your normal direction to complete the wing.

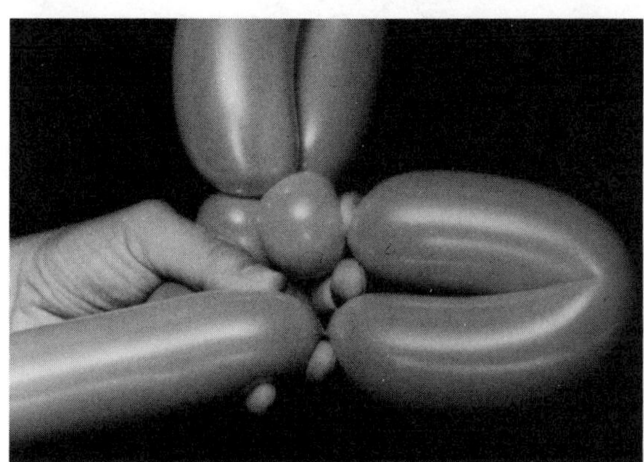

3 To make the tail, form a 1-inch bubble and a 3-inch loop. Lock twist the ends of the loop.

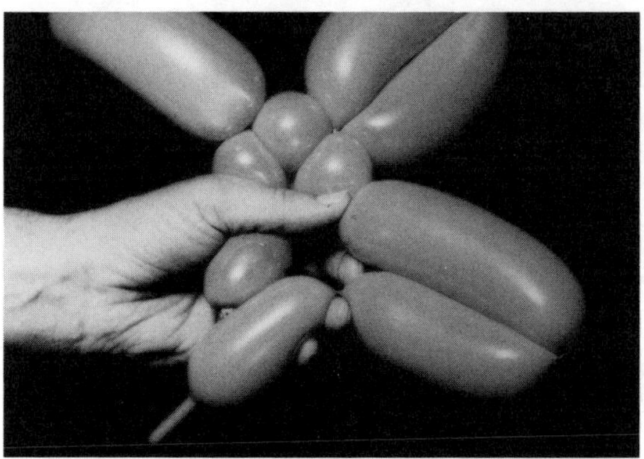

4 To make the second wing, form a 1-inch bubble, a 3-inch bubble, and a 4-inch bubble.

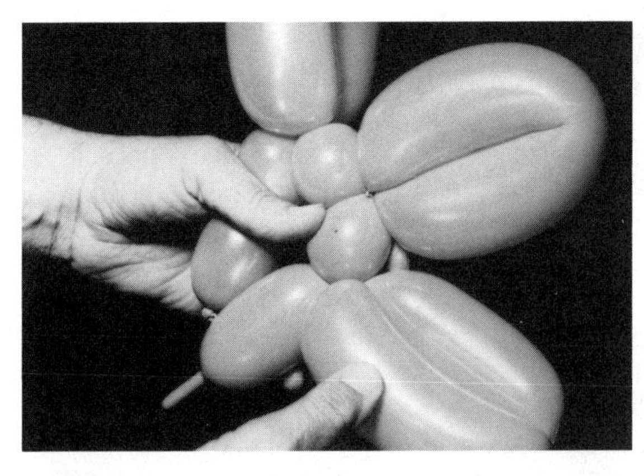

5 Lock twist the 3-inch and 4-inch bubbles together at the base to complete the second wing.

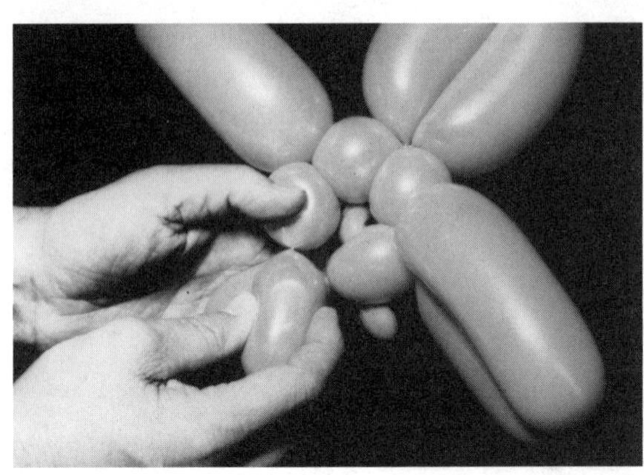

6 Form a 1-inch bubble and lock twist it at the base of the 1½-inch bubble made in step one.

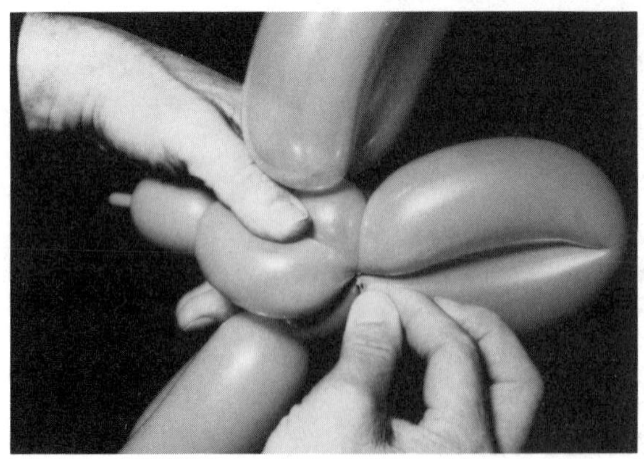

7 Stretch the 1½-inch bubble to the rear and wrap the knot end around the twist at the base of the tail to complete the body.

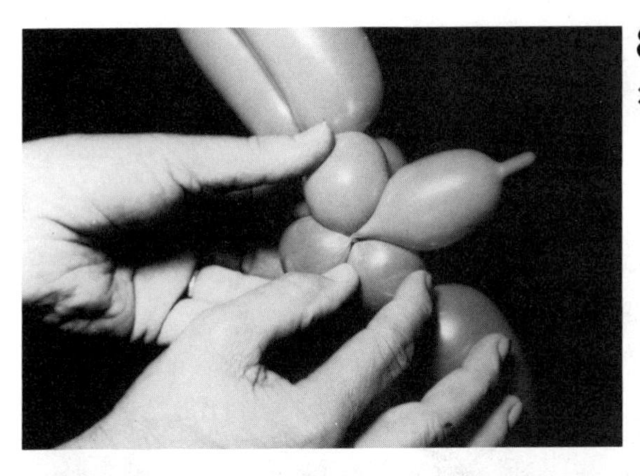

8 To hold the bird upright, wedge the rest of the balloon between the two adjacent 1-inch bubbles.

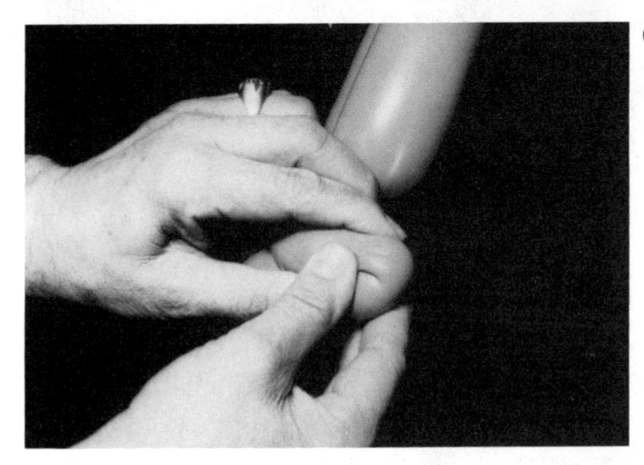

9 To make the head and beak, hold the uninflated tip of the balloon alongside the neck. Squeeze the neck with both hands until the air is forced into the uninflated tip.

EAGLE

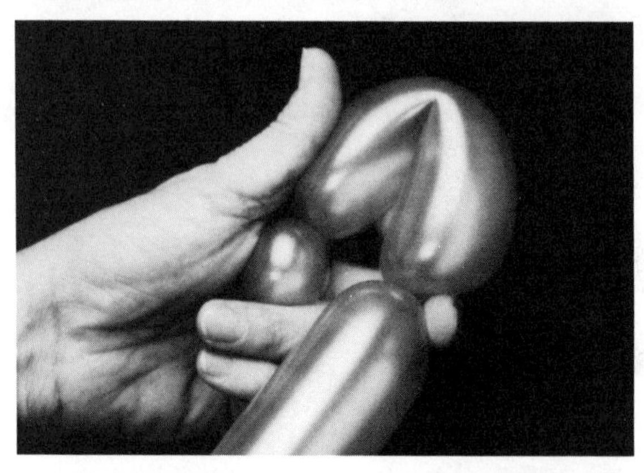

1 Inflate the balloon, leaving a 6-inch uninflated end. Tie a knot. Hold the balloon in your left hand with the uninflated end pointing right. To make the tail, form a 1-inch bubble and a 1½-inch loop. Lock twist the ends of the loop.

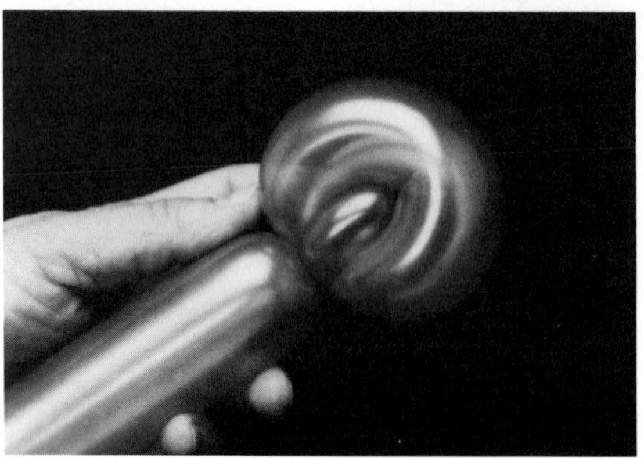

2 Tuck the 1-inch bubble inside the 1½-inch loop to complete the tail.

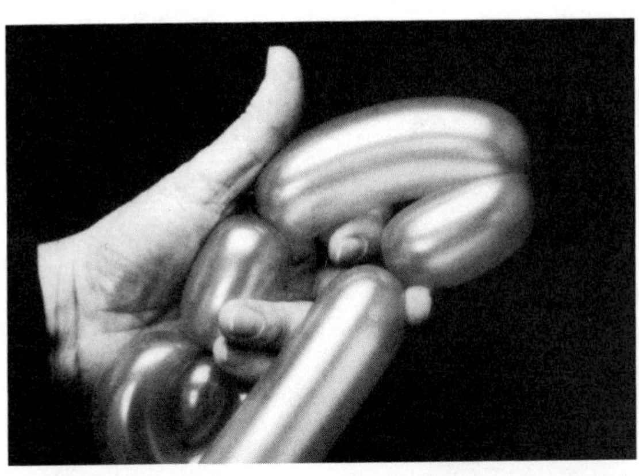

3 Form a 2-inch bubble for the body. To make one wing, form a 4-inch bubble and a 2-inch bubble and lock twist them at the base.

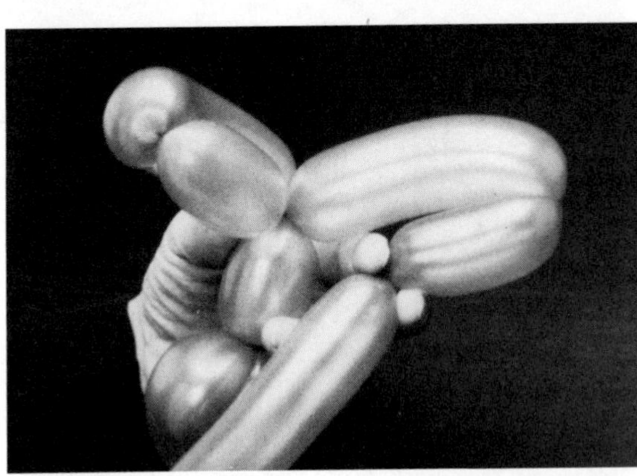

4 To make the other wing, form a 4-inch bubble and a 2-inch bubble, and lock twist them at the base.

5 To make the legs, form a five-bubble pinch and pop series with a 1-inch bubble, three ½-inch bubbles, and a 1-inch bubble. Lock twist the two 1-inch bubbles at the base.

6 To make the feet, pinch twist the first and third ½-inch bubbles of the leg assembly. Pop the second ½-inch bubble to separate the legs.

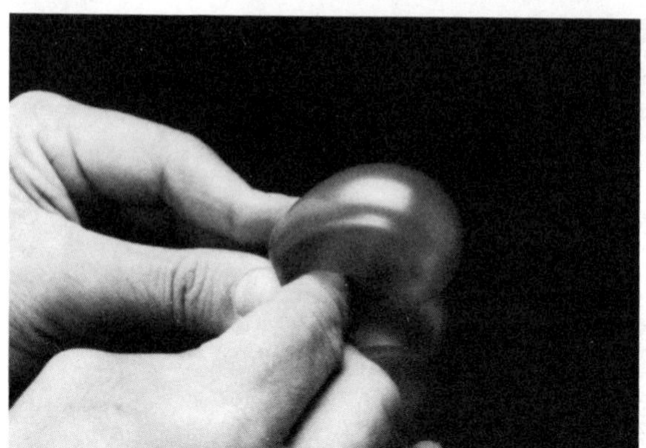

7 To make the head and beak, hold the uninflated tip of the balloon alongside the neck. Squeeze the neck with both hands until the air is forced into the uninflated tip.

TURKEY

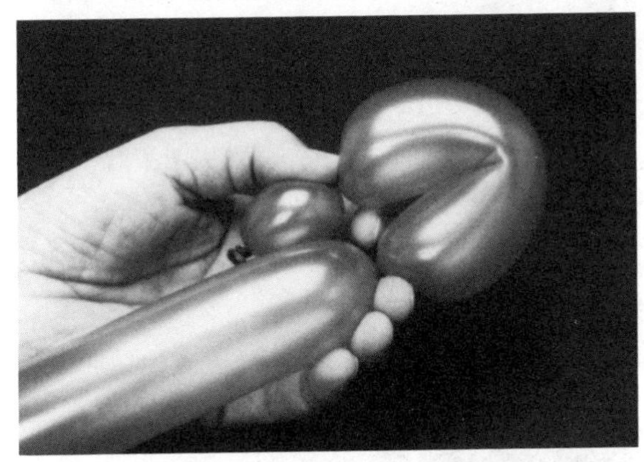

1 Inflate the balloon, leaving a 6-inch uninflated end. Tie a knot. Hold the balloon in your left hand with the uninflated end pointing right. To make the tail, form a 1-inch bubble and a 2-inch loop.

2 Lock twist the two ends of the loop, then tuck the 1-inch bubble inside it to complete the tail.

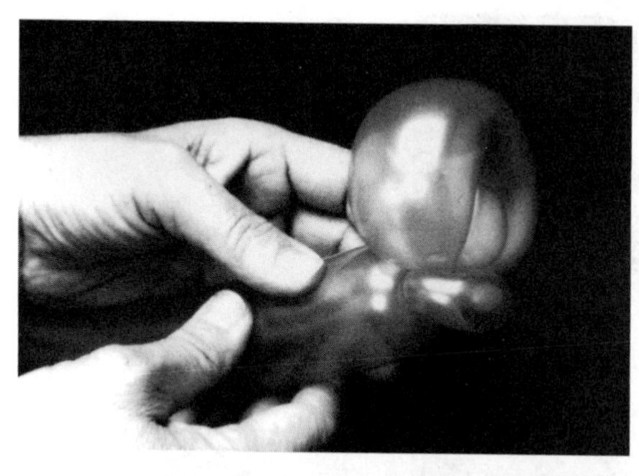

3 To hold the tail upright, form a 1-inch bubble and pinch twist it at the base of the tail.

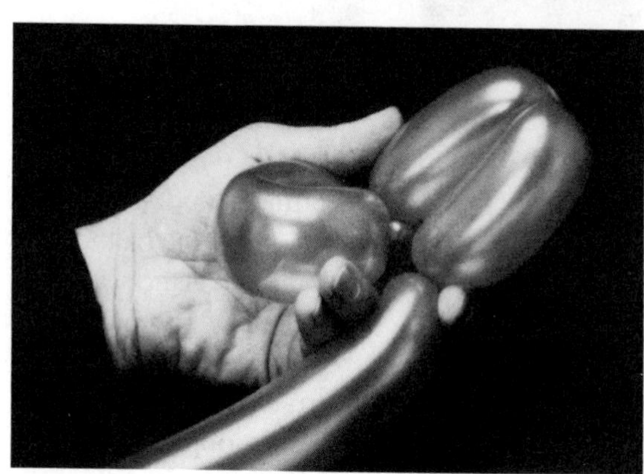

4 To make the body, form two 3-inch bubbles and lock twist them at the base.

5 To make the legs, form a chain of a 1½-inch bubble, a 1-inch bubble, three ½-inch bubbles, and a 1-inch bubble. Lock twist the two 1-inch bubbles at the base.

6 To complete the body and hold the neck upright, form a 1½-inch bubble.

7 Wedge the end of this 1½-inch bubble and the base of the rest of the balloon between the ends of the two 3-inch bubbles formed in step four.

8 To make the feet, pinch twist the first and third ½-inch bubbles of the leg assembly.

9 Pop the second ½-inch bubble to separate the legs.

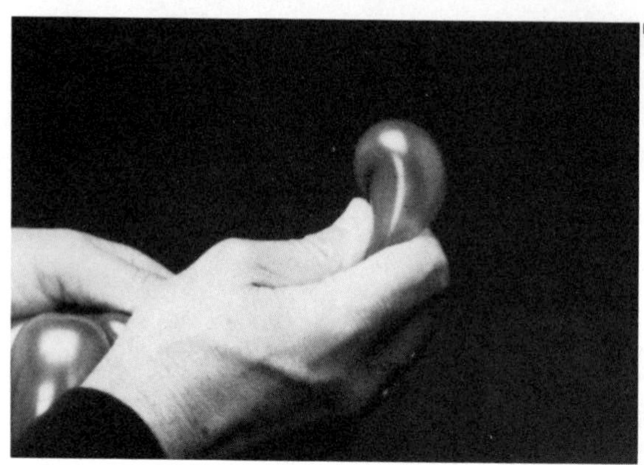

10 To make the head and beak, hold the tip of the uninflated part of the balloon down alongside the neck. Squeeze the neck with both hands until air is forced into the uninflated tip.

ROAD RUNNER

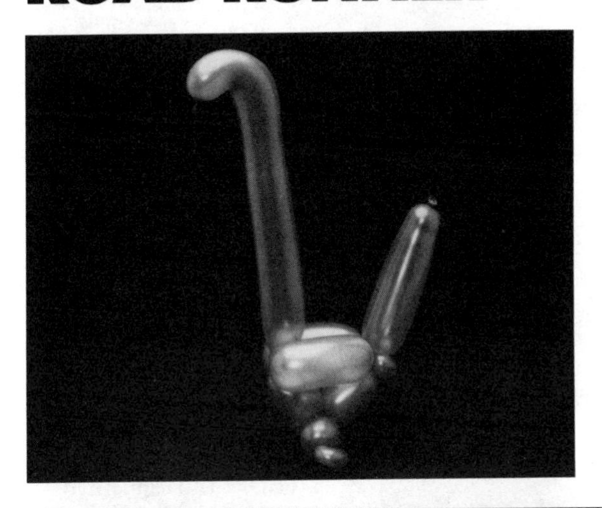

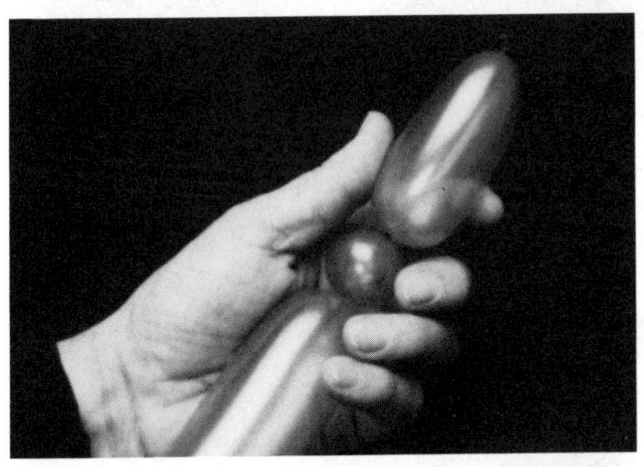

1 Inflate the balloon, leaving a 6-inch uninflated end. Tie a knot. Hold the balloon in your left hand with the uninflated end pointing right. To make the tail, form a 2½-inch bubble and a ¾-inch bubble.

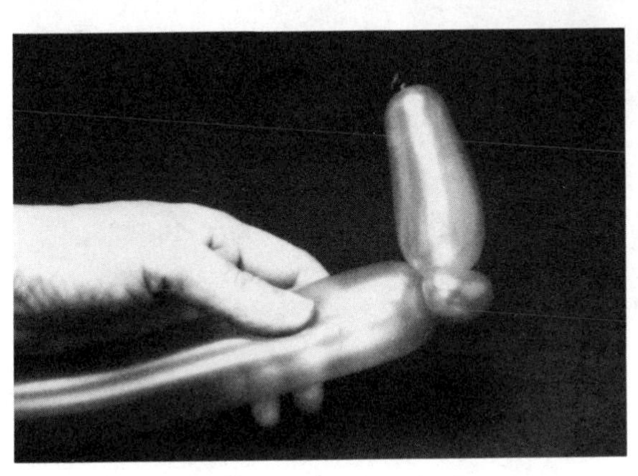

2 Pinch twist the ¾-inch bubble to hold the tail upright.

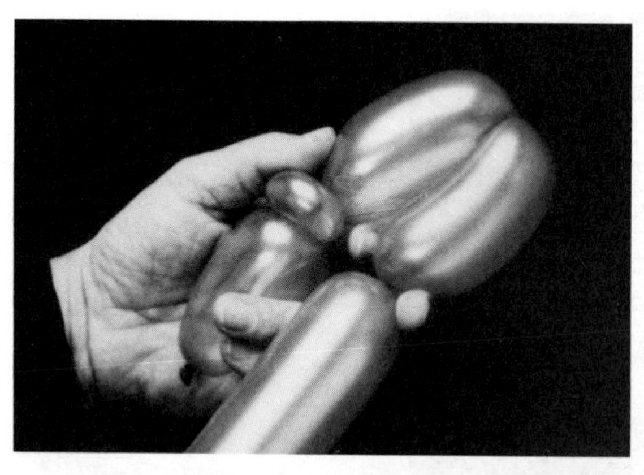

3 To make the body, form two 2½-inch bubbles and lock twist them at the base.

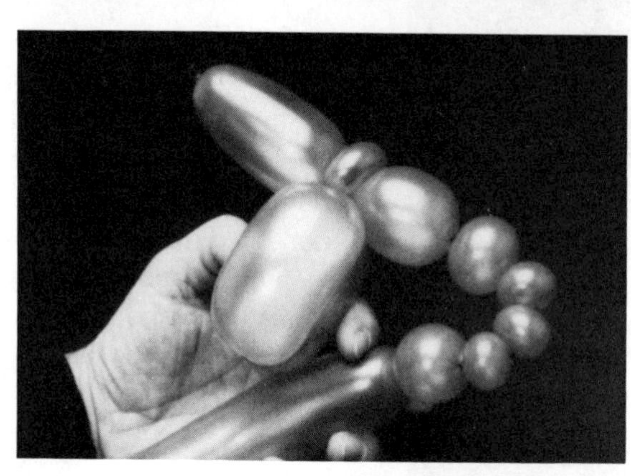

4 To make the legs, form a chain of a 1½-inch bubble, a 1-inch bubble, three ½-inch bubbles, and a 1-inch bubble. Lock twist the two 1-inch bubbles at the base.

5 To complete the body and hold the neck upright, form a 1-inch bubble. Wedge this bubble and the base of the rest of the balloon between the ends of the two 2½-inch bubbles formed in step three.

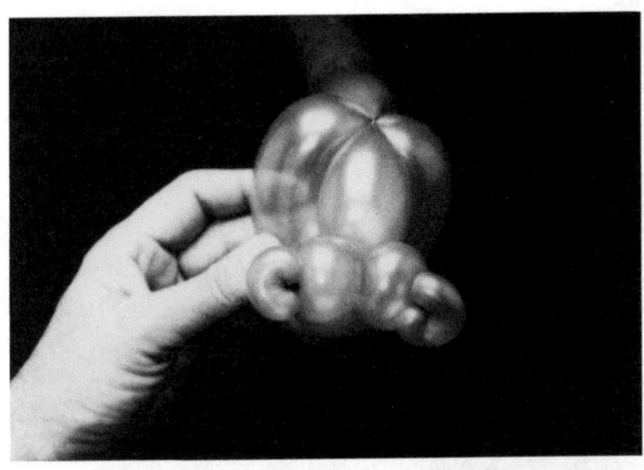

6 To make the feet, pinch twist the first and third ½-inch bubbles of the leg assembly. Pop the second ½-inch bubble to separate the legs.

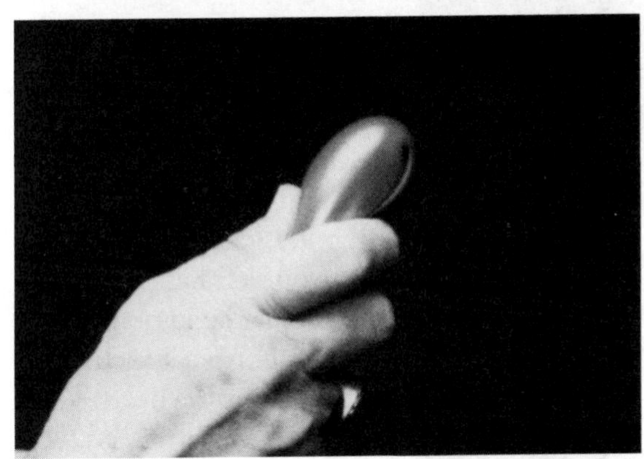

7 To make the head and beak, hold the uninflated tip of the balloon alongside the neck. Squeeze the neck with both hands until the air is forced into the uninflated tip.

TURTLE

1 Inflate the balloon, leaving a 4-inch uninflated end. Tie a knot. Hold the balloon in your left hand with the uninflated end pointing right. Form a 1-inch bubble for the head. To begin the body, form two 4-inch bubbles and lock twist them at the base.

2 Form another 4-inch bubble and hold it alongside the two-bubble lock twist formed in step one.

3 Roll the two 4-inch bubbles over the single 4-inch bubble, while pushing the single 4-inch bubble between them to complete the body.

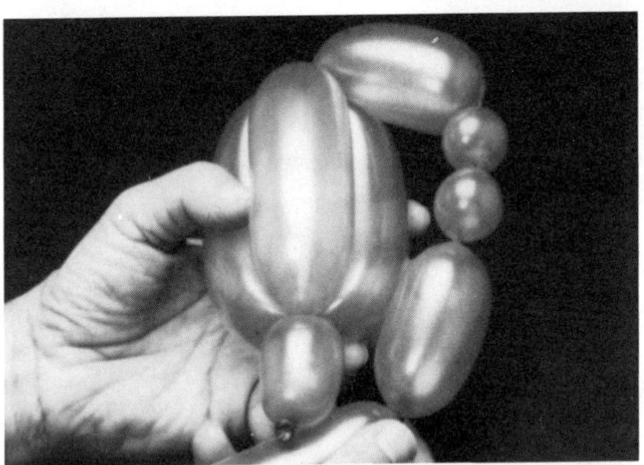

4 To make the legs on one side, form a chain of a 2-inch bubble, two ½-inch bubbles, and a 2-inch bubble. Lock twist the base of the last 2-inch bubble with the base of the head.

5 To make the legs on the other side, form a chain of a 2-inch bubble, two ½-inch bubbles, and a 2-inch bubble. Lock twist the rest of the balloon where the body and back legs join. Wrap the last bubble between one leg and the body to make the tail.

ALLIGATOR

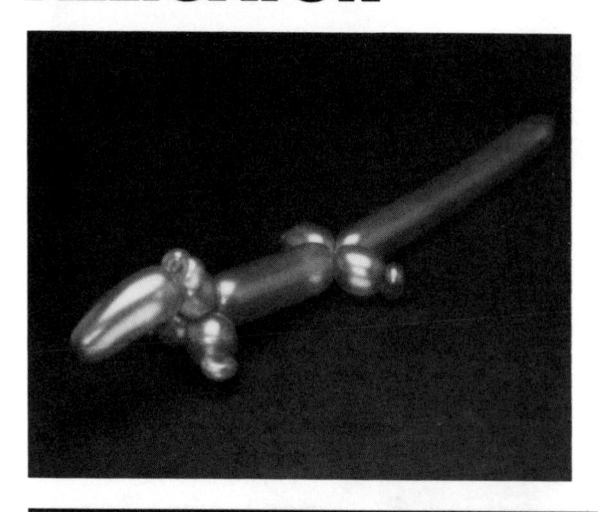

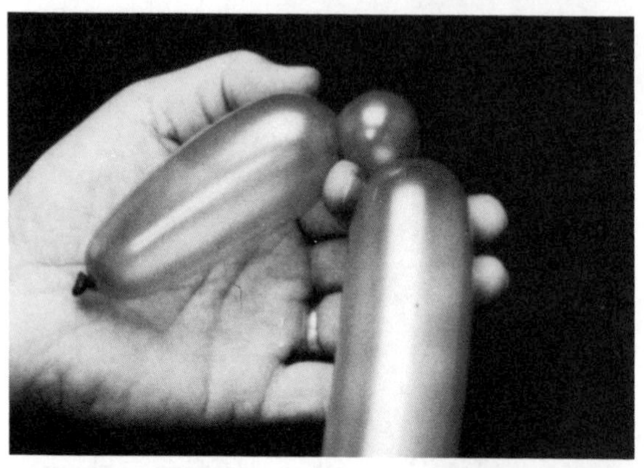

1 Inflate the balloon, leaving a 6-inch uninflated end. Tie a knot. Hold the balloon in your left hand with the uninflated end pointing right. Form a 3-inch bubble for the head, then a 1-inch bubble.

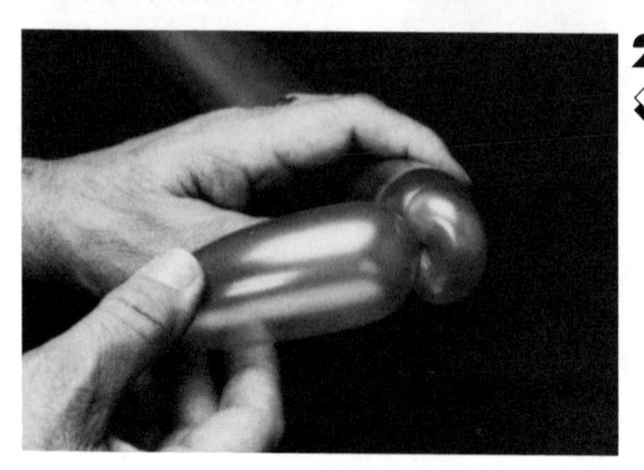

2 Pinch twist the 1-inch bubble to begin the eyes.

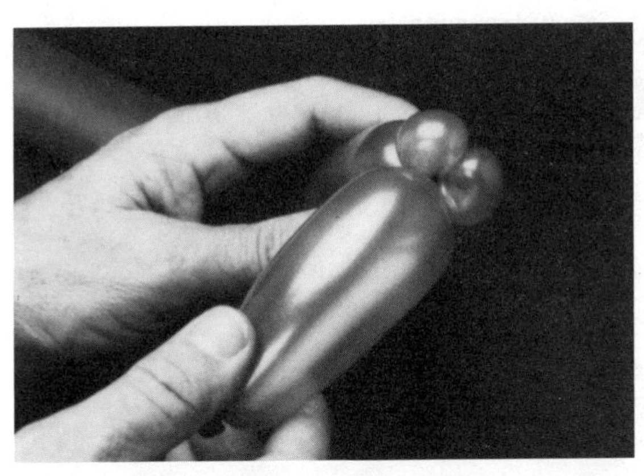

3 Twist the pinch-twisted bubble in half, twisting each half three or four times to complete the eyes.

4 Form a 1-inch bubble for the neck. To make the front legs, form a five-bubble pinch and pop series with a 1-inch bubble, three ½-inch bubbles, and a 1-inch bubble. Lock twist the second and third 1-inch bubbles at the base.

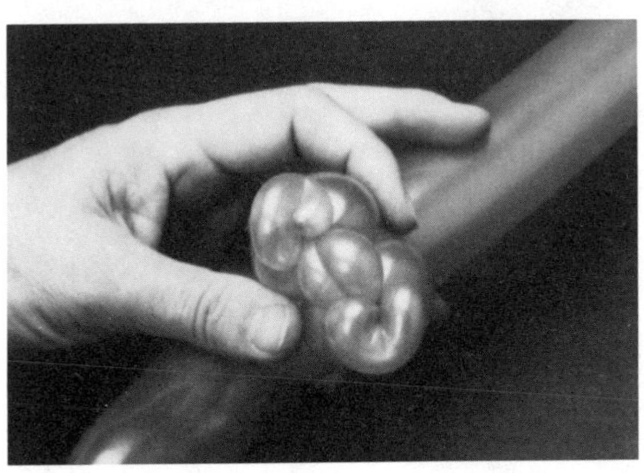

5 To make the front feet, pinch twist the first and third ½-inch bubbles, twisting each at least four times. Pop the second ½-inch bubble to separate the front legs.

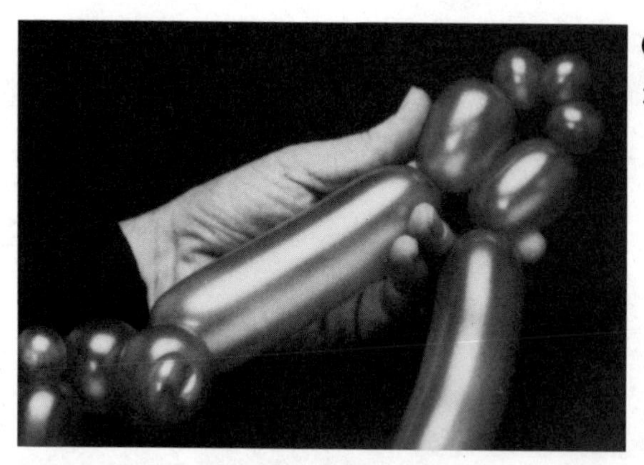

6 Form a 5-inch bubble for the body. To make the back legs, form a five-bubble pinch and pop series with a 1-inch bubble, three ½-inch bubbles, and a 1-inch bubble. Lock twist the two 1-inch bubbles at the base.

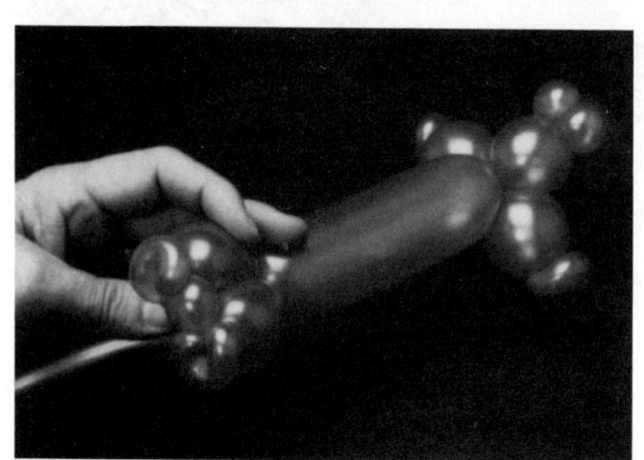

7 To make the back feet, pinch twist the first and last ½-inch bubbles, twisting each at least four times. Pop the second ½-inch bubble to separate the back legs and complete the figure.

FROG

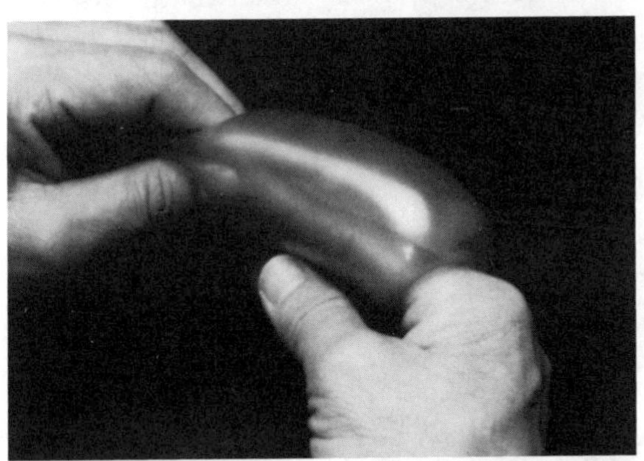

1 Inflate the balloon, leaving an 8-inch uninflated end. Tie a knot. Hold the balloon in your left hand with the uninflated end pointing left. To begin the body, form a 3-inch tulip twist at the knot end of the balloon.

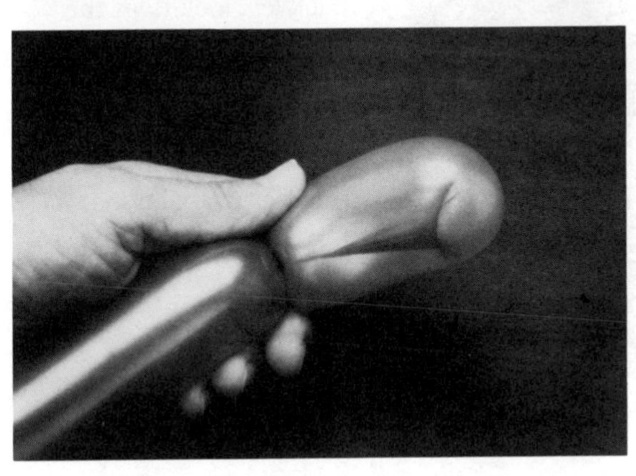

2 Leave the tulip twist offset (as illustrated).

3 To begin the legs, form a chain of a 1-inch bubble, a ¾-inch bubble, two 1-inch bubbles, a ¾-inch bubble and a 1-inch bubble. Lock twist the first and last 1-inch bubbles.

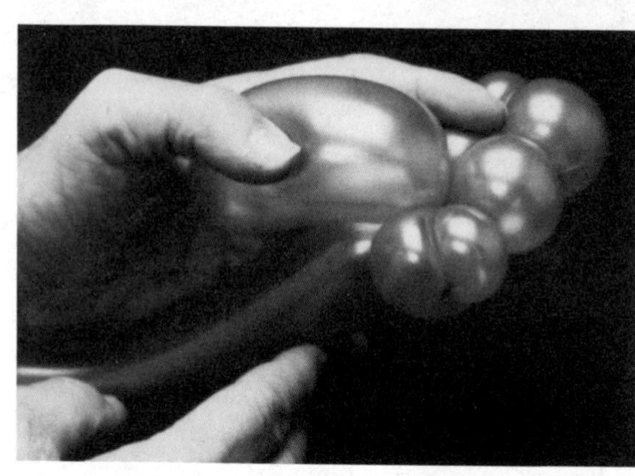

4 To complete one back leg, lock twist the first 1-inch bubble and the first ¾-inch bubble at the base.

5 To complete the other back leg, lock twist the fourth 1-inch bubble and the second ¾-inch bubble at the base, twisting each at least four times. (The middle two balloons will form the front legs.)

6 To make the eyes, form a small bubble at the end of the 3-inch tulip twist, twisting it at least four times.

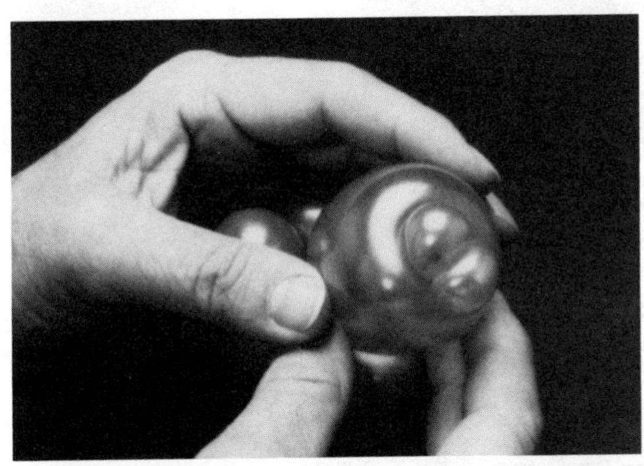

7 Twist this small bubble in half, twisting each half three or four times to complete the eyes.

8 Position the body over the front legs, with the eyes on top of the body to complete the figure. Remove the remaining inflated portion of the balloon by popping it.

BULLFROG

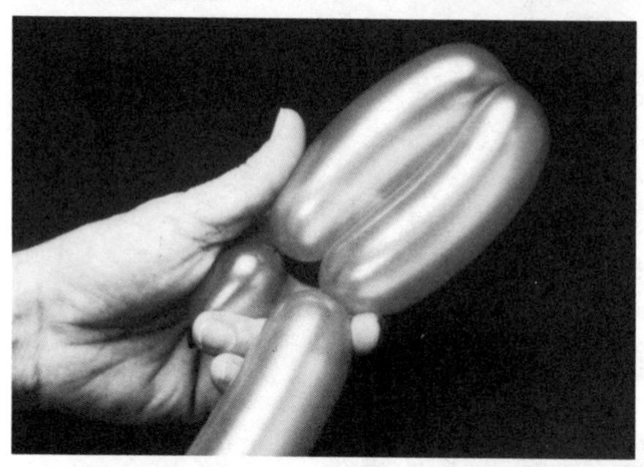

1 Inflate the balloon, leaving an 8-inch uninflated end. Tie a knot. Hold the balloon in your left hand with the uninflated end pointing right. Form a 1-inch bubble for the head. To begin the body, form two 3-inch bubbles and lock twist them at the base.

2 To make the front legs, form a chain of a 1-inch bubble, a ½-inch bubble, a ¾-inch bubble, three ½-inch bubbles, a ¾-inch bubble, a ½-inch bubble, and a 1-inch bubble. Lock twist the two 1-inch bubbles at the base.

3 Pinch twist the first and fifth ½-inch bubbles to make the joints of the front legs.

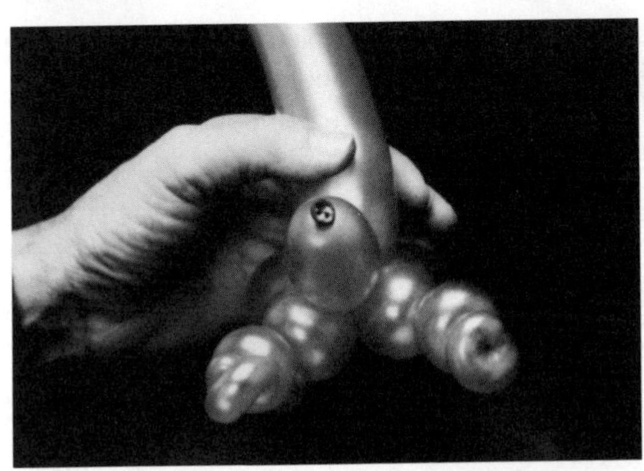

4 To complete the front legs, pinch twist the second and fourth ½-inch bubbles, twisting each at least four times. Pop the third ½-inch bubble to separate the front legs.

5 To make the eyes, form a ¾-inch bubble at the base of the head and pinch twist it. Twist the pinch-twisted bubble in half, twisting each half three or four times.

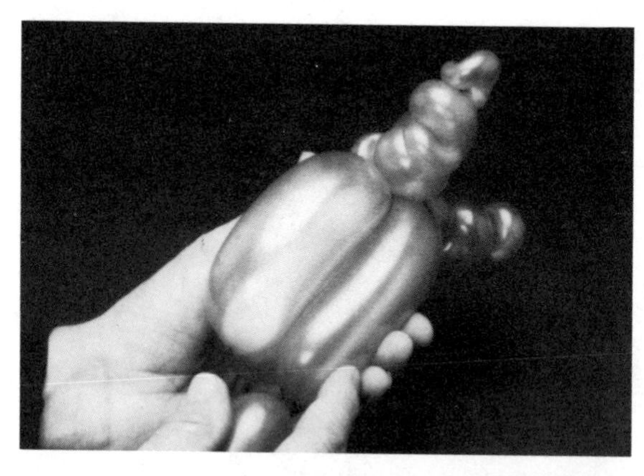

6 To complete the body, form a 3-inch bubble and hold it alongside and beneath the two 3-inch bubbles formed in step one.

7 Roll the two 3-inch bubbles over the single 3-inch bubble, while pushing the single 3-inch bubble between them.

8 To make the back legs, form a chain of a 1½-inch bubble, a ½-inch bubble, a 1-inch bubble, three ½-inch bubbles, a 1-inch bubble, a ½-inch bubble, and a 1½-inch bubble. Lock twist the two 1½-inch bubbles at the base.

9 Pinch twist the first and fifth ½-inch bubbles to make the joints in the back legs.

10 To complete the back legs, pinch twist the second and fourth ½-inch bubbles, twisting each at least four times. Pop the third ½-inch bubble to separate the back legs and complete the figure. The uninflated tip of the balloon becomes the tail.

FISH

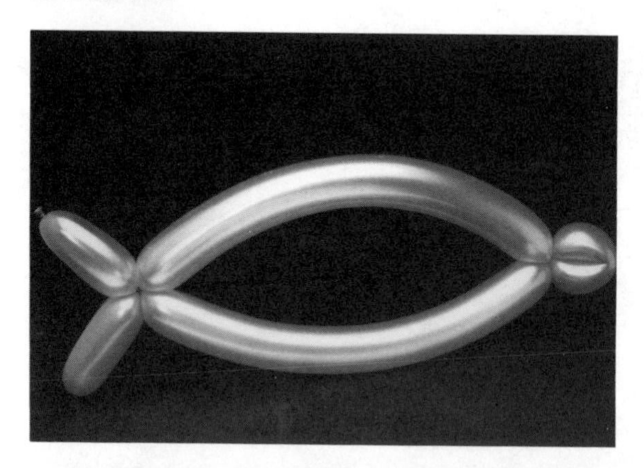

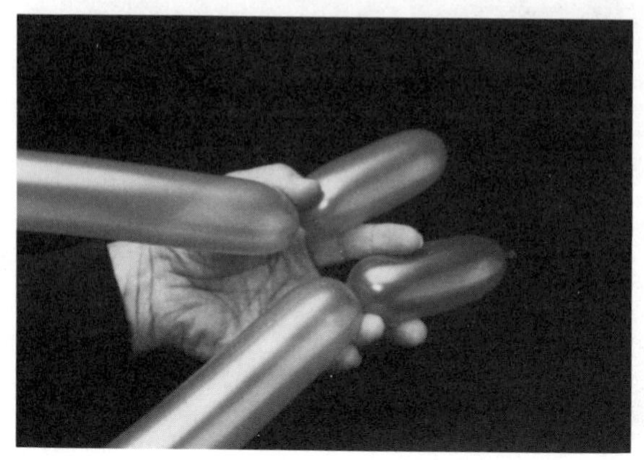

1 Inflate the balloon all the way and allow a small amount of air to escape to soften it. Tie a knot. Form a 3-inch bubble at each end of the balloon.

2 Lock twist these two bubbles at the base to make the tail fins.

3 Pinch the balloon to form a 2-inch loop opposite the tail fins. Lock twist the ends of this loop to make the mouth and complete the figure.

KISSING FISH

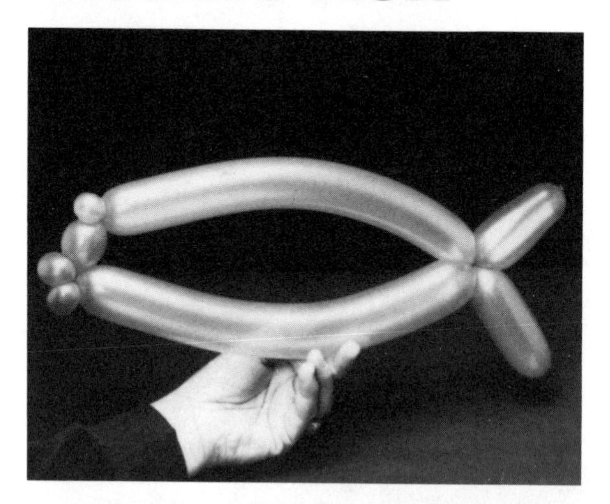

1 Inflate the balloon all the way, then allow a fairly large amount of air to escape to soften it. Tie a knot. Fold the balloon to find the middle point and twist it. Form two 1-inch bubbles on one side of the middle twist.

2 Pinch twist these two 1-inch bubbles to make the mouth.

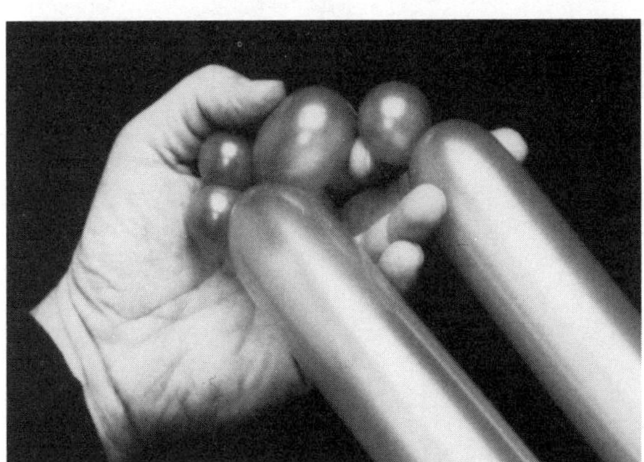

3 To make the head and eyes, form a 1-inch bubble and a ½-inch bubble on the opposite side of the middle twist.

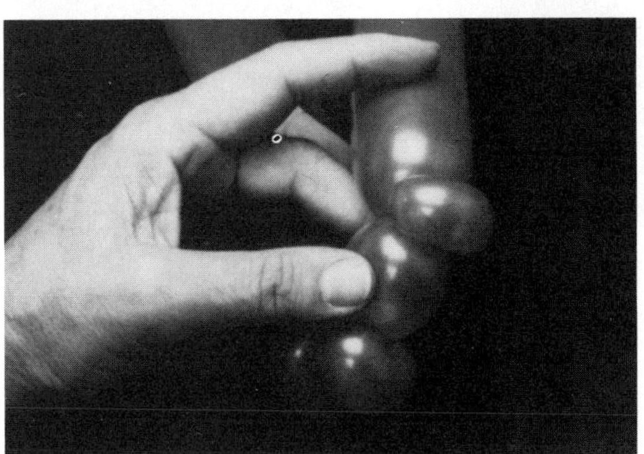

4 Pinch twist the ½-inch bubble.

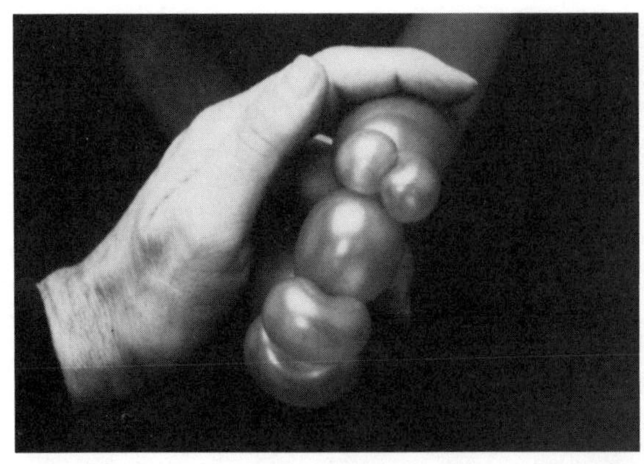

5 ◇ Twist the pinch-twisted bubble in half, twisting each half three or four times to complete the eyes.

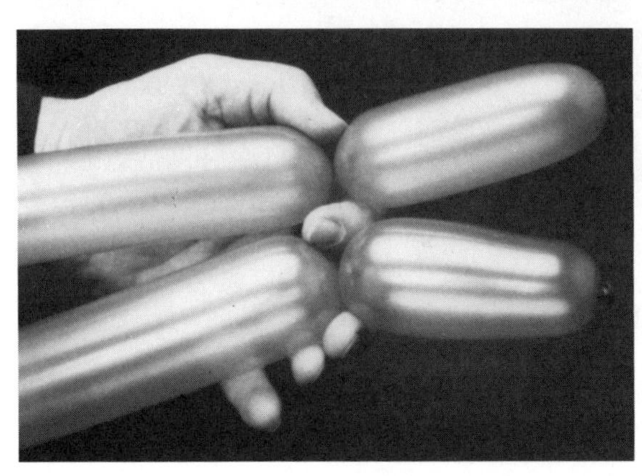

6 ◇ To make the tail fins and complete the figure, form a 3-inch bubble at each end of the balloon and lock twist them at the base.

Figures other than animals can easily be formed using the same basic twists shown so far. The following figures are among those I've developed through the years. Master them, and you'll soon be able to create interesting new designs of your own.

SWORD

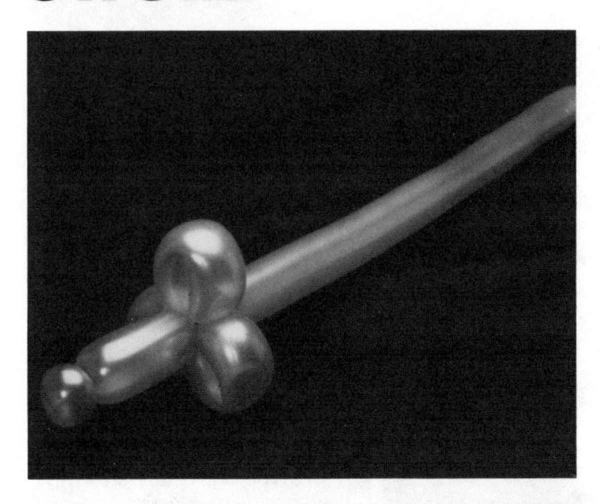

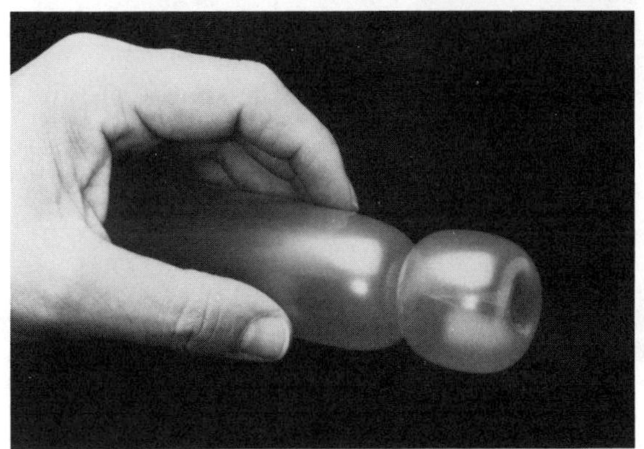

1 Inflate the balloon, leaving a 2-inch uninflated end. Tie a knot. Hold the balloon in your left hand with the uninflated end pointing left. To begin the handle, form a 1-inch tulip twist at the knot end of the balloon.

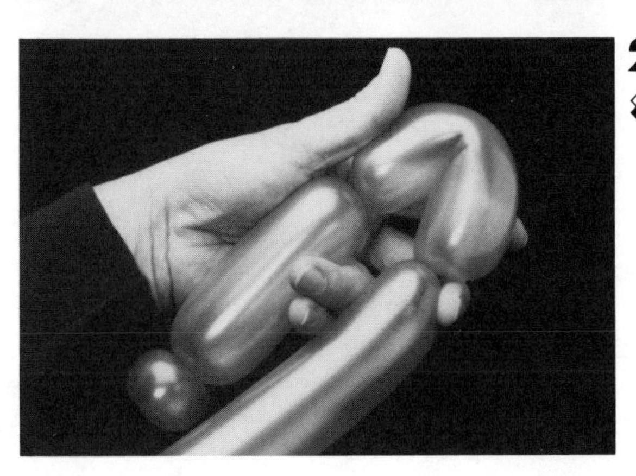

2 Hold the balloon in your left hand with the uninflated end pointing right. To complete the handle, form a 4-inch bubble. To make the first section of the handguard, form a 2-inch loop and lock twist the ends.

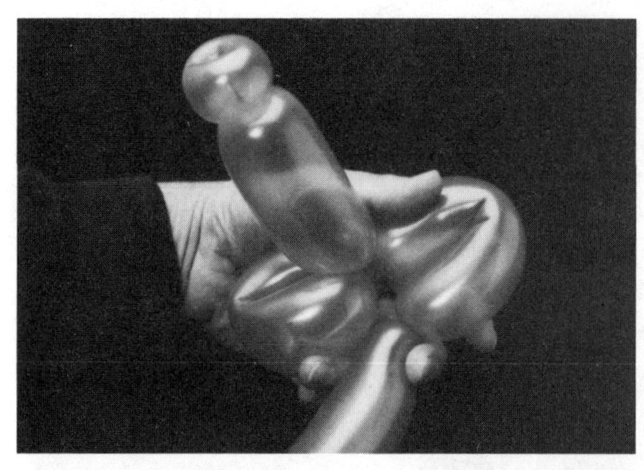

3 Form a second 2-inch loop. Lock twist the ends of this loop to make the second section of the handguard.

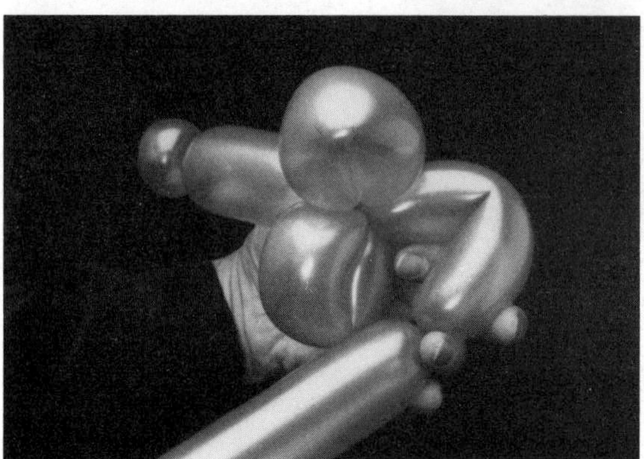

4 Form a third 2-inch loop and lock twist the ends to complete the handguard and the figure. The remaining balloon forms the blade of the sword.

SKI POLE

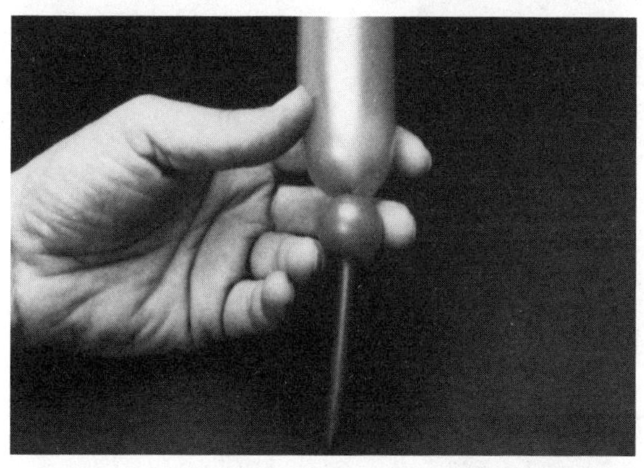

1 Inflate the balloon, leaving a 3-inch uninflated end. Allow a small amount of air to escape before tying the knot. Hold the balloon in your left hand with the uninflated end pointing right. Form a ½-inch bubble next to the uninflated tip of the balloon.

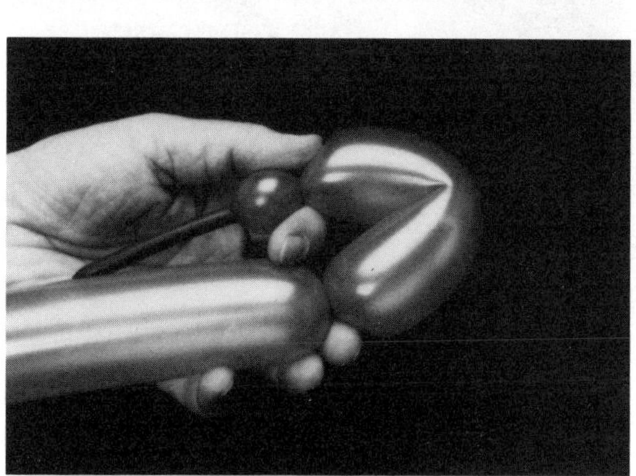

2 To make the first section of the basket, form a 2-inch loop and lock twist the ends.

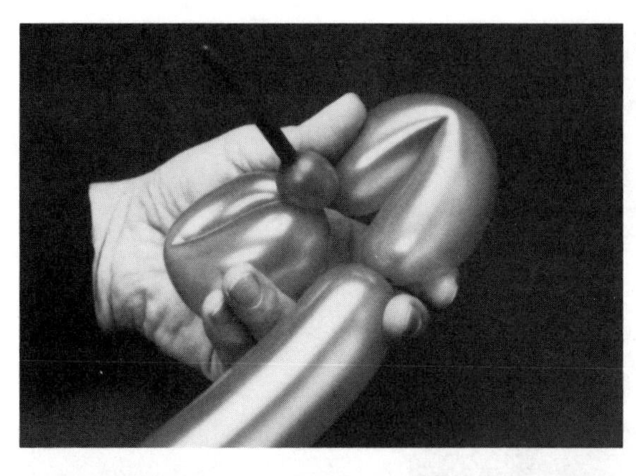

3 Form a second 2-inch loop and lock twist the ends to make the second section of the basket.

4 Form a third 2-inch loop and lock twist the ends to complete the basket.

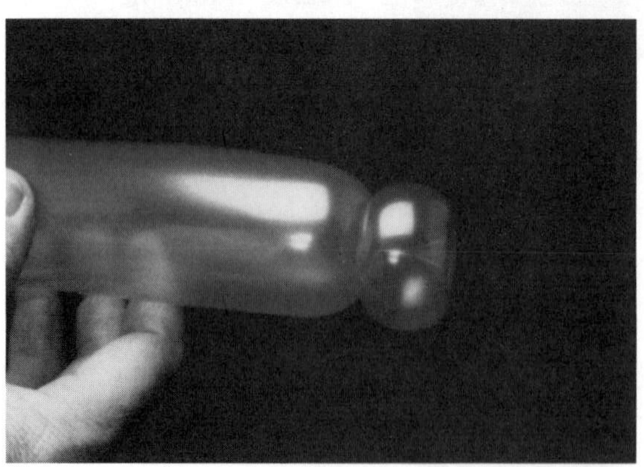

5 Form a 1-inch tulip twist at the knot end of the balloon to complete the figure.

PISTOL

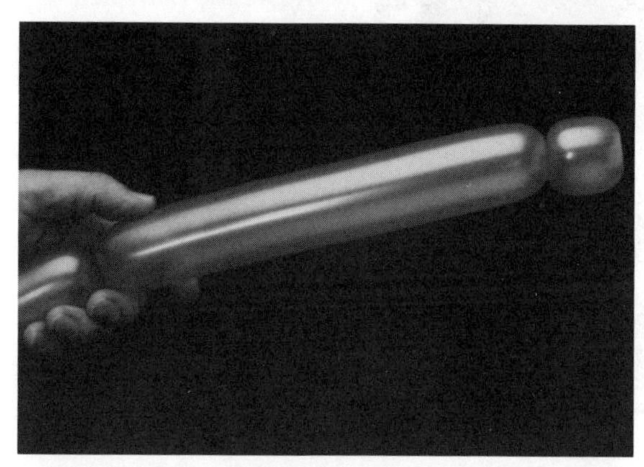

1 Inflate the balloon, leaving a 6-inch uninflated end. Tie a knot. Hold the balloon in your left hand with the uninflated end pointing left. To make the barrel, form a 1-inch tulip twist at the knot end of the balloon, then an 8-inch bubble.

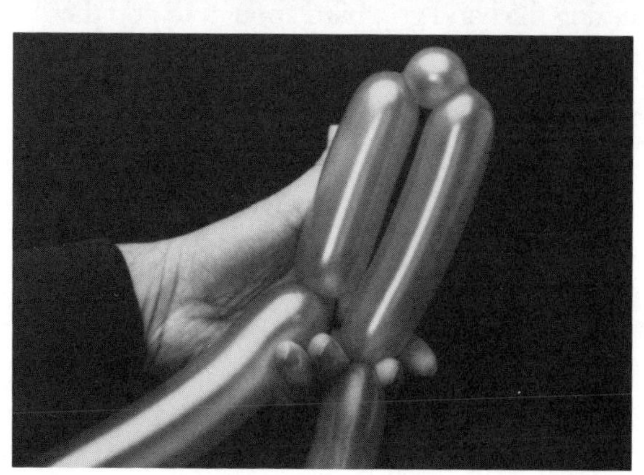

2 Hold the 8-inch bubble in your left hand with the uninflated end pointing right. To make the hand grip and hammer, form a 4-inch bubble, a 1-inch bubble, and a 5-inch bubble. Lock twist the 4-inch bubble and the 5-inch bubble at the base. Make sure the 5-inch bubble ends up at the rear of the hand grip.

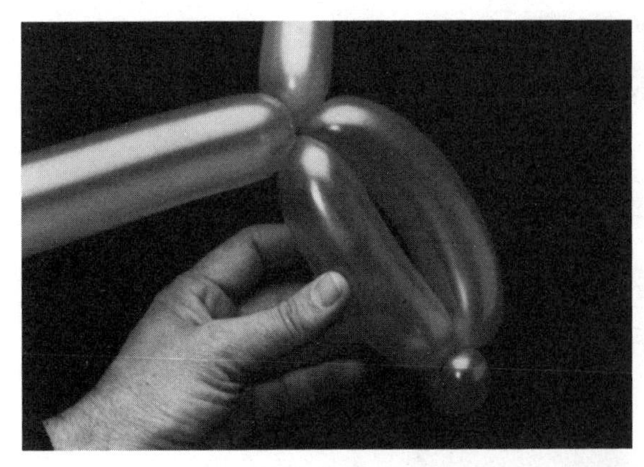

3 Pinch twist the 1-inch bubble at the end of the hand grip, twisting it at least five times.

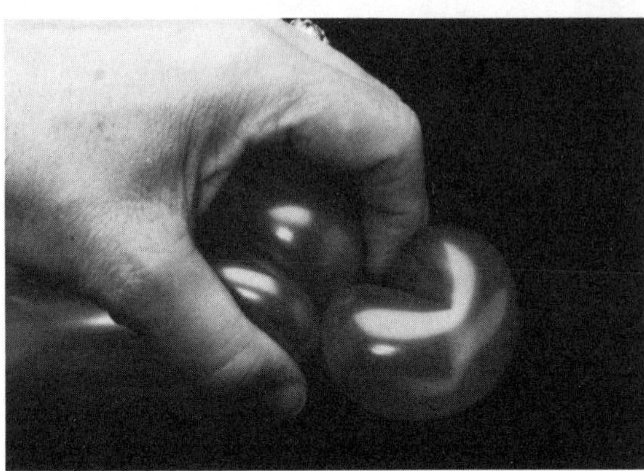

4 To make the hammer, form a 1-inch loop where the hand grip joins the barrel. Lock twist the ends of the loop, twisting it at least five times. To complete the pistol, remove the remaining inflated portion of the balloon by popping it.

The pistol can be "fired" by squeezing the hand grip hard enough to pop the two bubbles that form it.

HEADPHONES

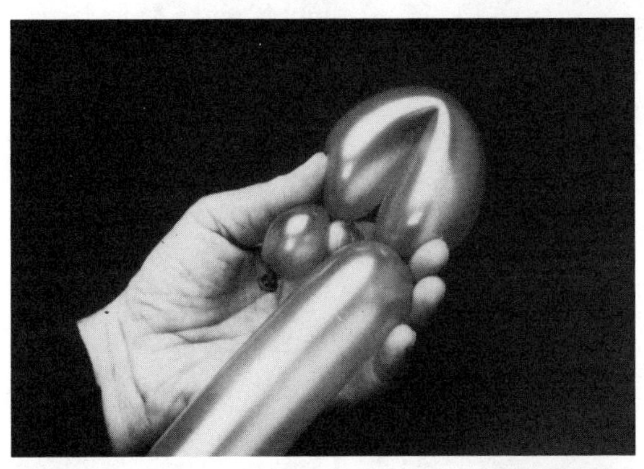

1 Inflate the balloon, leaving a 6-inch uninflated end. Tie a knot. Hold the balloon in your left hand with the uninflated end pointing right. To make one earpiece, form a 1-inch bubble and a 1½-inch loop. Lock twist the two ends of the loop.

2 Tuck the 1-inch bubble inside the 1½-inch loop to complete the earpiece.

3 To begin the headpiece, form a 1-inch bubble and a ½-inch bubble. Pinch twist the ½-inch bubble.

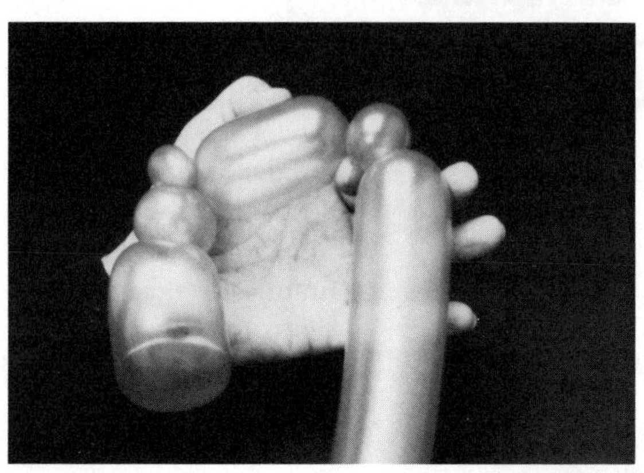

4 Next, form a 2-inch bubble and a ½-inch bubble. Pinch twist the ½-inch bubble.

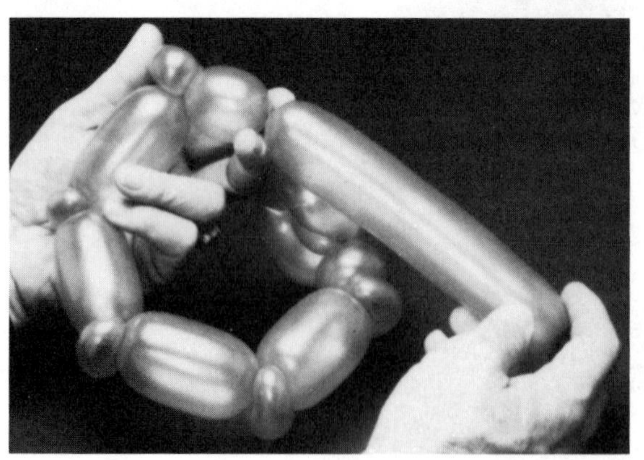

5 Continue forming 2-inch bubbles followed by ½-inch pinch-twisted bubbles until about 5 inches of inflated balloon remains.

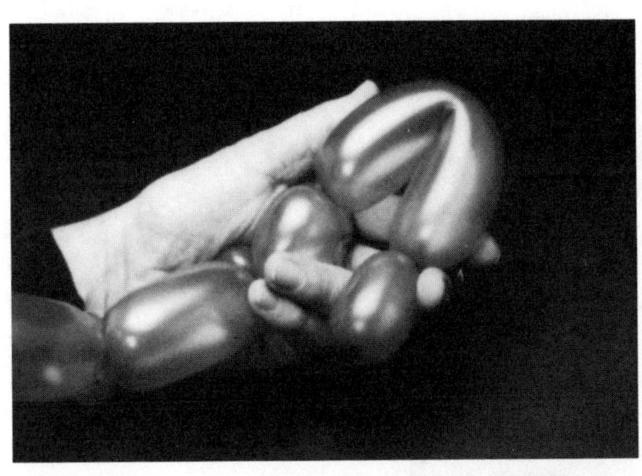

6 To make the second earpiece, form a 1-inch bubble, then a 1½-inch loop. Lock twist the two ends of the loop.

7 Tuck the remaining end of the balloon inside the 1½-inch loop to finish the earpiece and complete the headphones.

SKATEBOARD

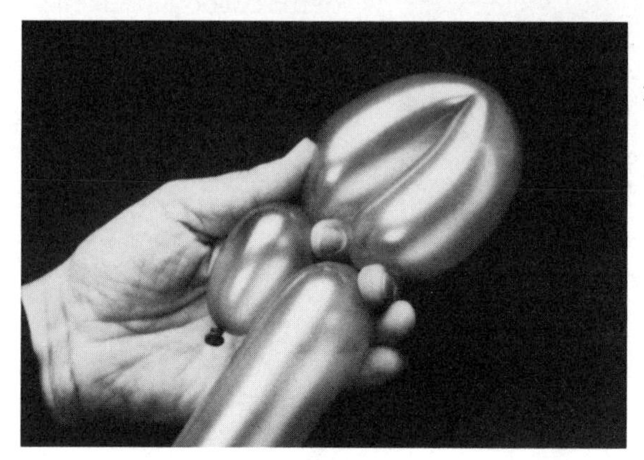

1 Inflate the balloon, leaving a 4-inch uninflated end. Tie a knot. Hold the balloon in your left hand with the uninflated end pointing right. To make one wheel, form a 1-inch bubble and a 2-inch loop. Lock twist the ends of the loop.

2 Tuck the 1-inch bubble inside the 2-inch loop to complete this wheel.

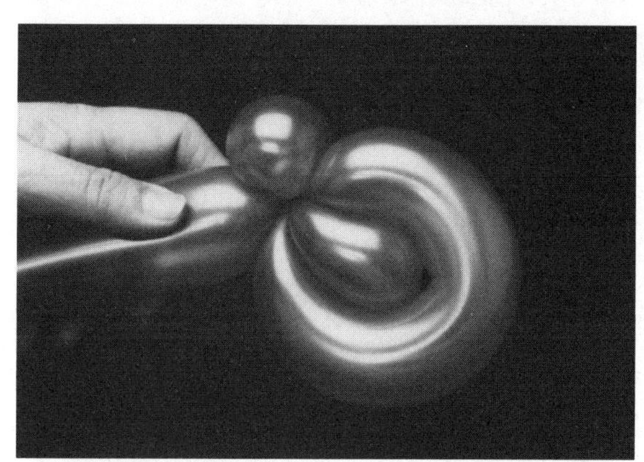

3 Form a 1-inch bubble and pinch twist it to hold the wheel in proper position.

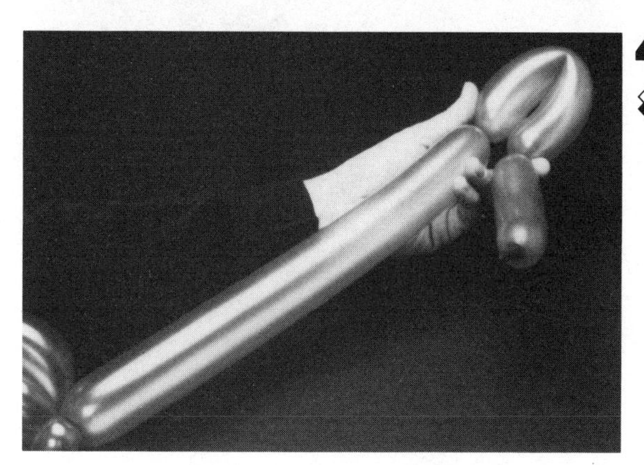

4 Form a 12-inch bubble for the board. To make the other wheel, form a 2-inch loop and lock twist the ends.

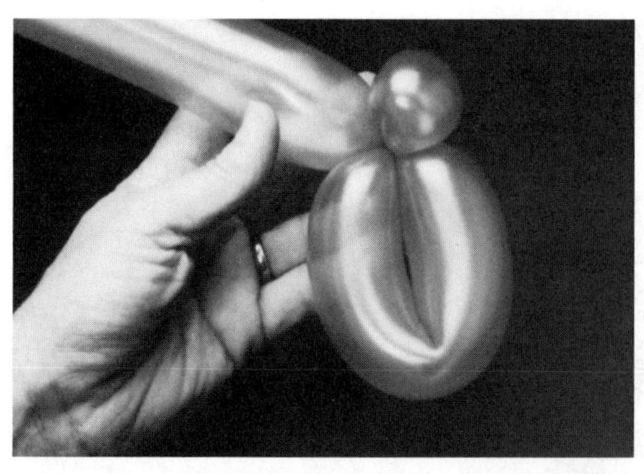

5 Form a 1-inch bubble. Pinch twist it to hold the wheel in proper position.

6 Tuck the remaining end of the balloon inside the 2-inch loop to finish the second wheel and complete the figure.

SCOOTER

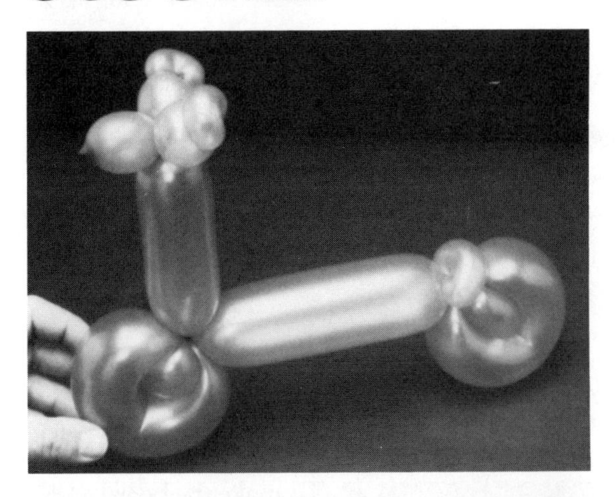

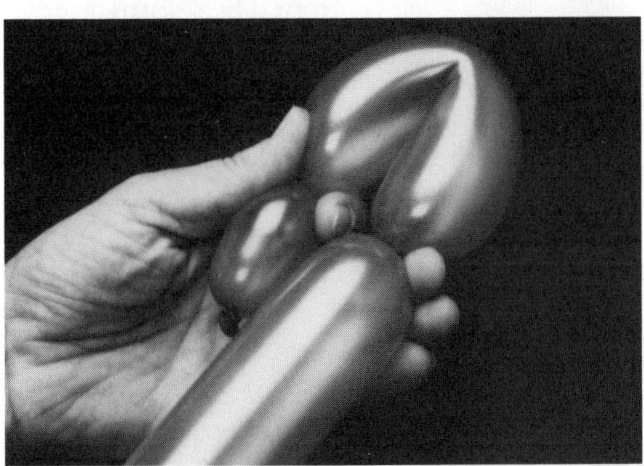

1 Inflate the balloon, leaving a 6-inch uninflated end. Tie a knot. Hold the balloon in your left hand with the uninflated end pointing right. To make the rear wheel, form a 1-inch bubble and a 2-inch loop. Lock twist the ends of this loop to make the rear wheel.

2 Tuck the 1-inch bubble inside the 2-inch loop to complete the rear wheel.

3 Form a 1-inch bubble and pinch twist it to hold the wheel in proper position.

4 To make the board and front wheel, form a 5-inch bubble and a 2-inch loop. Lock twist the ends of the loop.

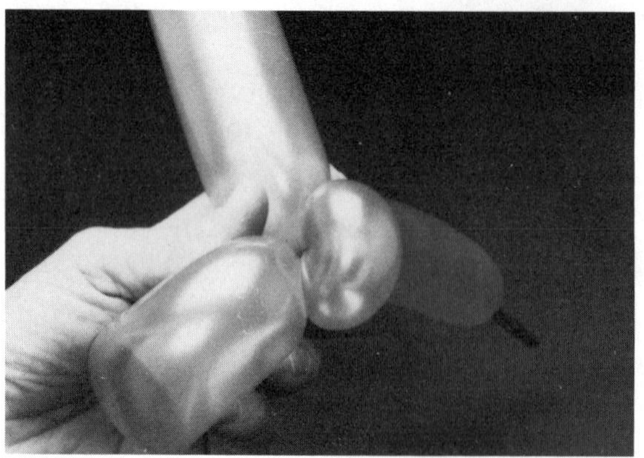

5 Form a 1-inch bubble and pinch twist it where the body joins the front wheel.

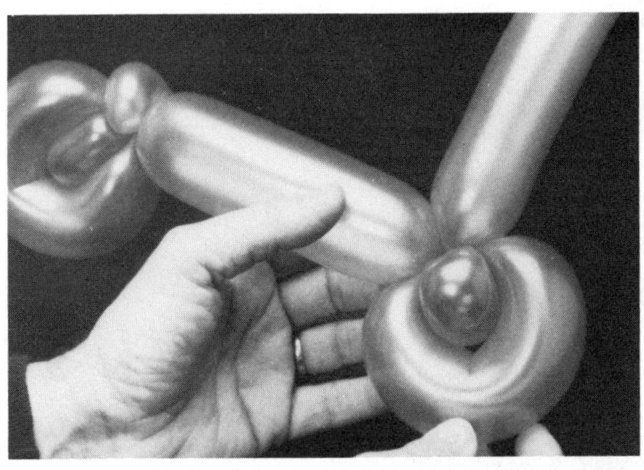

6 Tuck the pinch-twisted bubble inside the 2-inch loop to complete the front wheel.

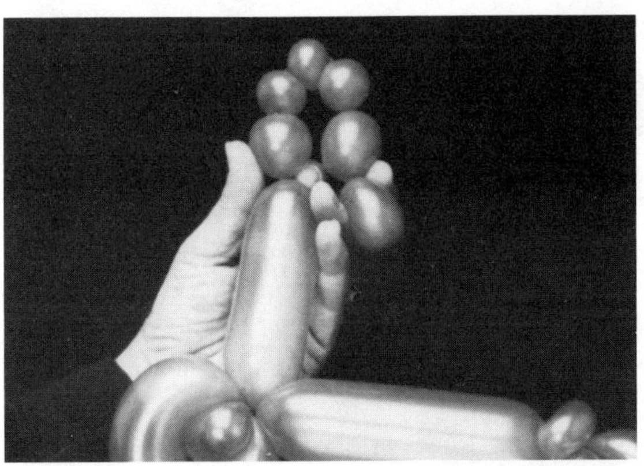

7 Form a 4-inch bubble for the upright. To make the handlebars, form a five-bubble pinch and pop series with a 1-inch bubble, three ½-inch bubbles, and a 1-inch bubble. Lock twist the two 1-inch bubbles at the base.

8 Pinch twist the first and last ½-inch bubbles, twisting each at least four times. Pop the second ½-inch bubble to separate the handlebars and complete the figure.

CHOPPER

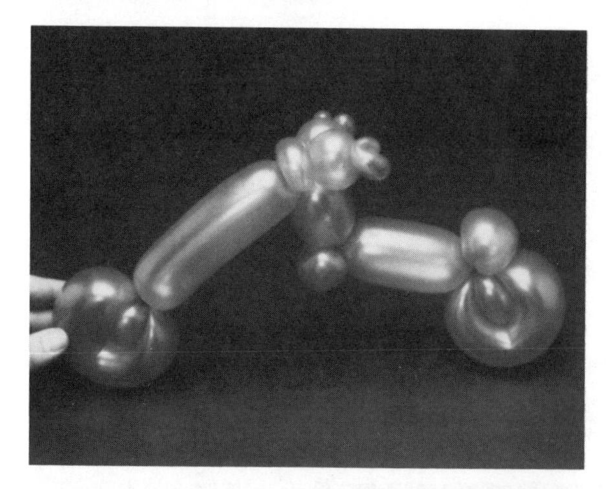

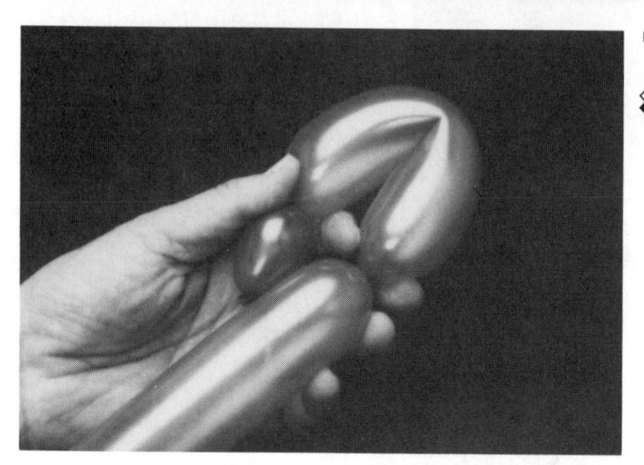

1 Inflate the balloon, leaving a 6-inch uninflated end. Tie a knot. Hold the balloon in your left hand with the uninflated end pointing right. To make the rear wheel, form a 1-inch bubble and a 2-inch loop. Lock twist the ends of the loop.

2 Tuck the 1-inch bubble inside the 2-inch loop to complete the rear wheel.

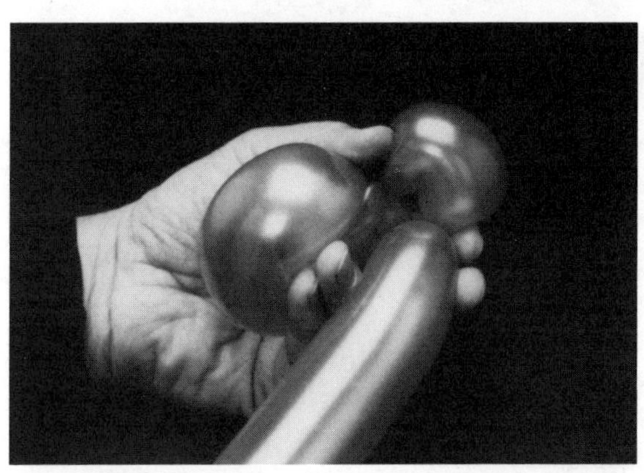

3 Form a 1-inch loop for the seat back.

4 Lock twist the ends of this loop to complete the seat and hold the rear wheel in proper position.

5 Form a 3-inch bubble for the frame. To make the motor, form a 1½-inch bubble and pinch twist it.

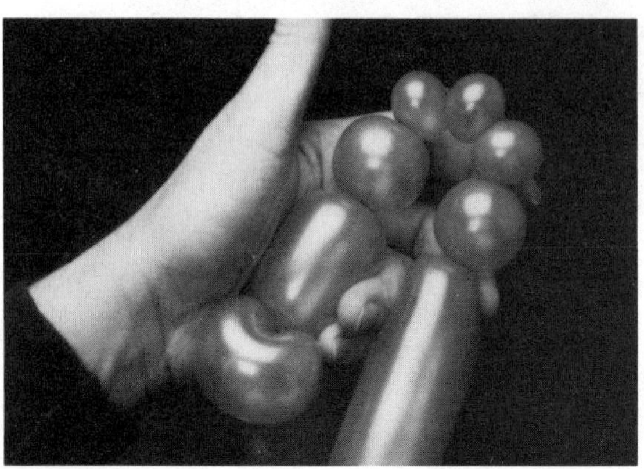

6 Form a 2-inch bubble for the upright. To make the handlebars, form a five-bubble pinch and pop series with a 1-inch bubble, three ½-inch bubbles, and a 1-inch bubble. Lock twist the two 1-inch bubbles at the base.

7 Form a 1-inch bubble and pinch twist it in front of the handlebars to hold them in proper position.

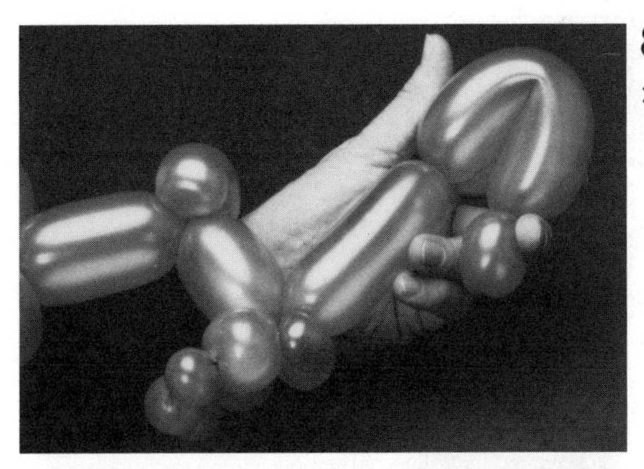

8 Form a 3-inch bubble for the front forks. To make the front wheel, form a 2-inch loop and lock twist the ends. Tuck the remaining end of the balloon inside the 2-inch loop.

9 Pinch twist the first and last ½-inch bubbles of the handlebar assembly, twisting each bubble at least four times. Pop the second ½-inch bubble to separate the handlebars and complete the figure.

BICYCLE

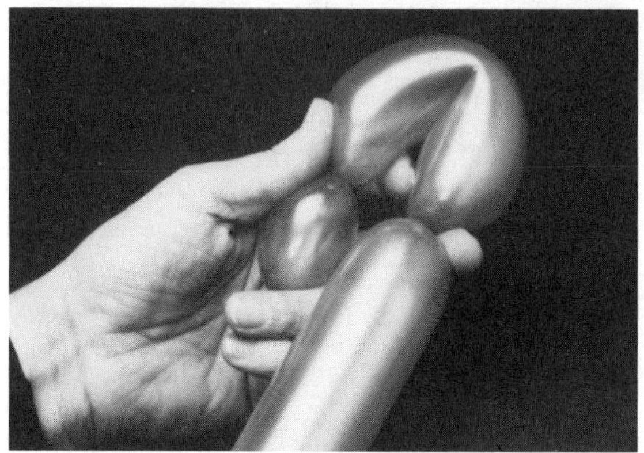

1 Inflate the balloon, leaving a 6-inch uninflated end. Tie a knot. Hold the balloon in your left hand with the uninflated end pointing right. To make the rear wheel, form a 1-inch bubble and a 2-inch loop. Lock twist the ends of the loop.

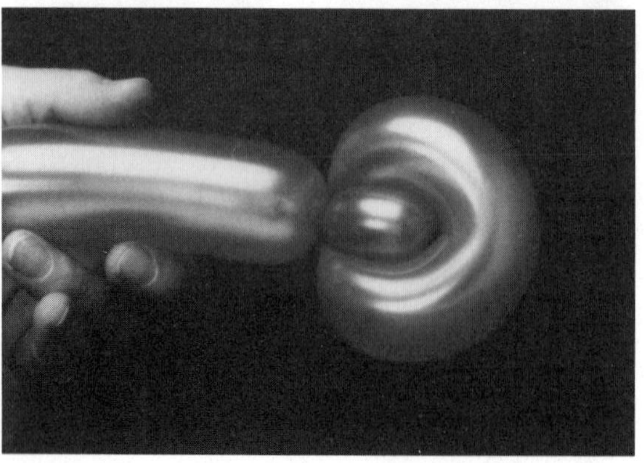

2 Tuck the 1-inch bubble inside the 2-inch loop to complete the rear wheel.

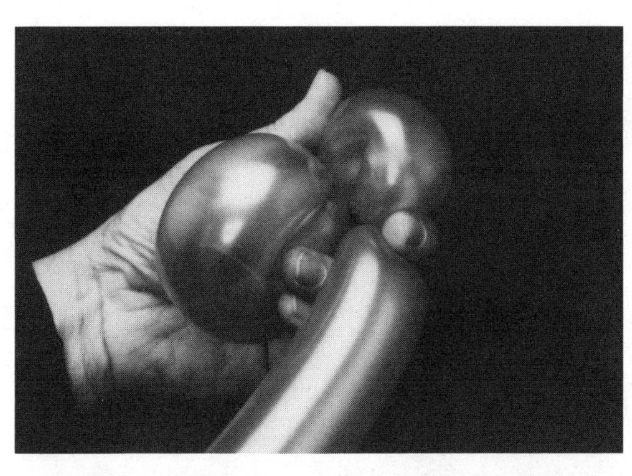

3 To make the back seat, form a 1-inch loop.

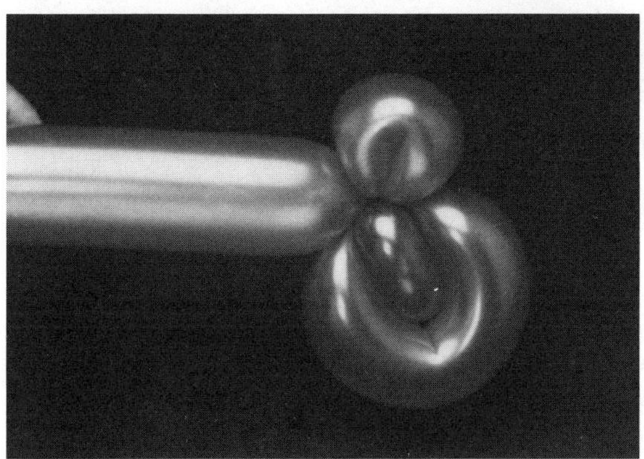

4 Lock twist the ends of this loop to complete the seat and hold the rear wheel in proper position.

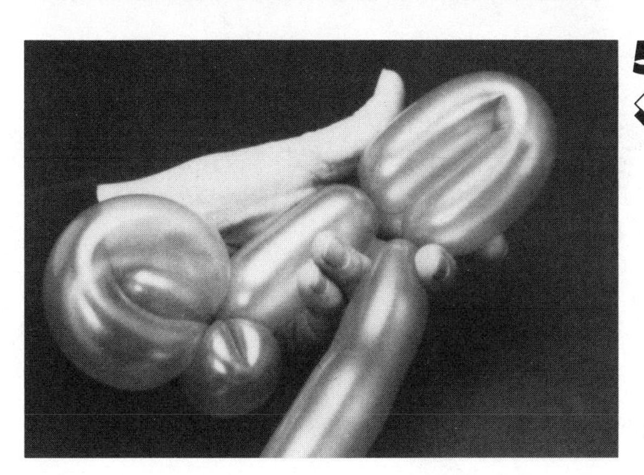

5 Form a 3-inch bubble for the frame. To make the front wheel, form a 2-inch loop and lock twist the ends.

6 Form a 1½-inch bubble for the upright. To make the handlebars, form a five-bubble pinch and pop series with a 1-inch bubble, three ½-inch bubbles, and a 1-inch bubble. Lock twist the two 1-inch bubbles at the base.

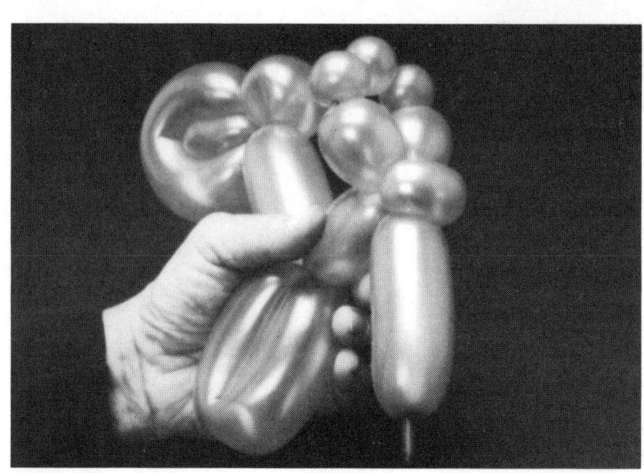

7 Form a 1-inch bubble and pinch twist it in front of the handlebars to hold them in proper position.

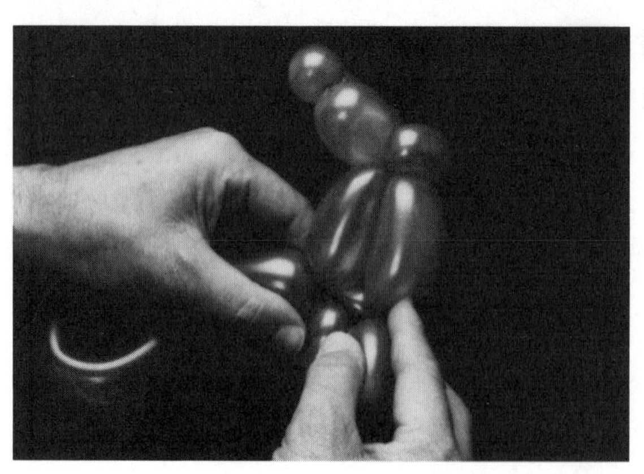

8 Form a 2-inch bubble to complete the upright.

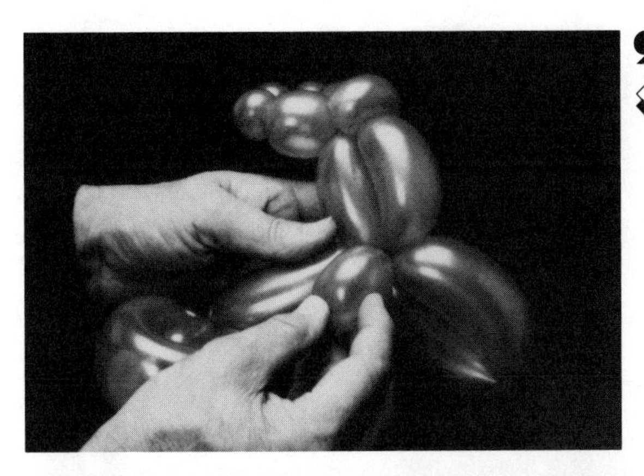

9 Lock twist the base of this bubble with the base of the upright (where it joins the front wheel). Tuck the rest of the balloon inside the 2-inch loop to complete the front wheel.

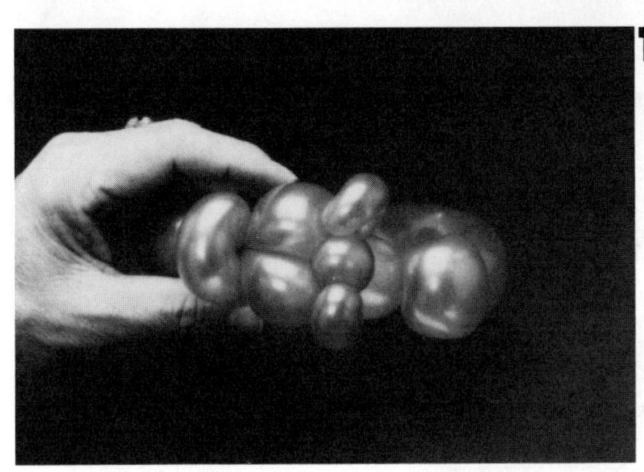

10 Pinch twist the first and last ½-inch bubbles of the handlebar assembly, twisting each bubble at least four times. Pop the second ½-inch bubble to separate the handlebars and complete the figure.

AIRPLANE

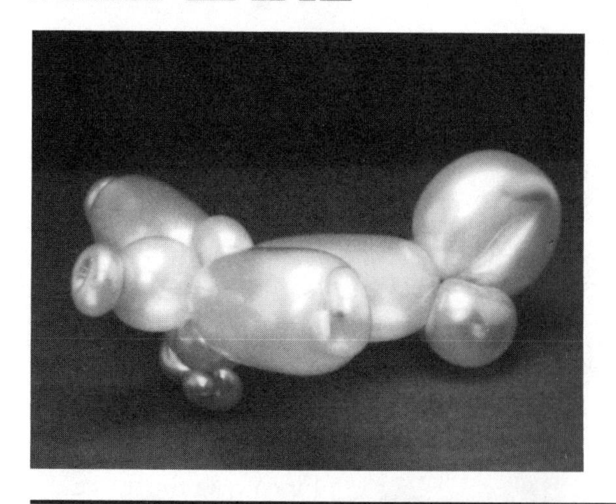

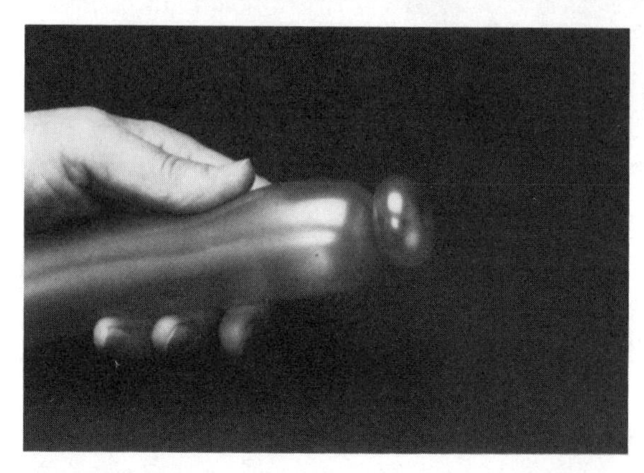

1 Inflate the balloon, leaving a 6-inch uninflated end. Tie a knot. Hold the balloon in your left hand with the uninflated end pointing left. Form a ½-inch tulip twist at the knot end to make the propeller.

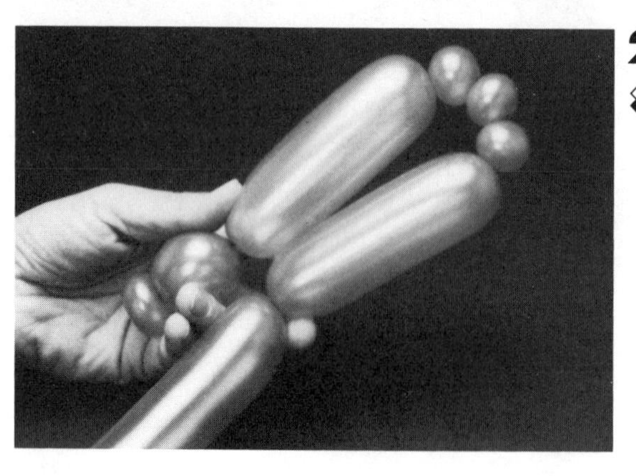

2 Hold the balloon in your left hand with the uninflated end pointing right. Form a 1-inch bubble for the nose. To make the wings, form a five-bubble pinch and pop series with a 4-inch bubble, three ½-inch bubbles, and a 4-inch bubble. Lock twist the two 4-inch bubbles at the base.

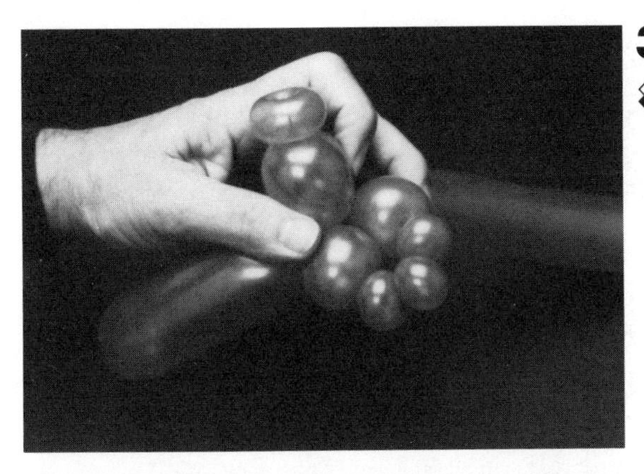

3 To make the landing gear, form a five-bubble pinch and pop series with a 1-inch bubble, three ½-inch bubbles and a 1-inch bubble. Lock twist the two 1-inch bubbles at the base.

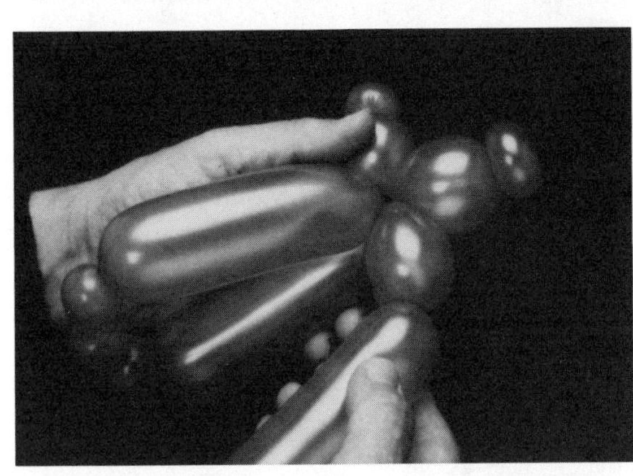

4 Form a 1-inch bubble for the cockpit.

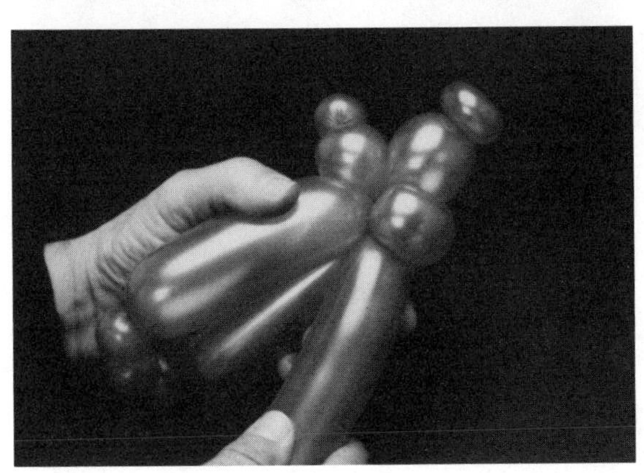

5 Pinch twist this bubble to complete the cockpit.

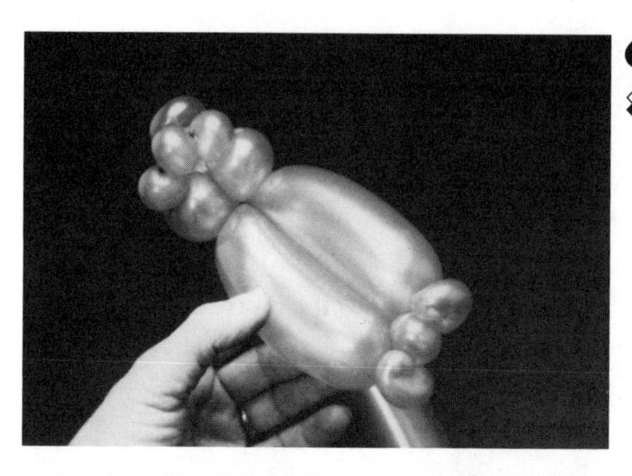

6 Pinch twist the first and last ½-inch bubbles of the wing assembly, twisting each bubble at least four times to complete the wings. Pop the second ½-inch bubble to separate the wings. Place the cockpit crosswise between the wings to hold them in proper position.

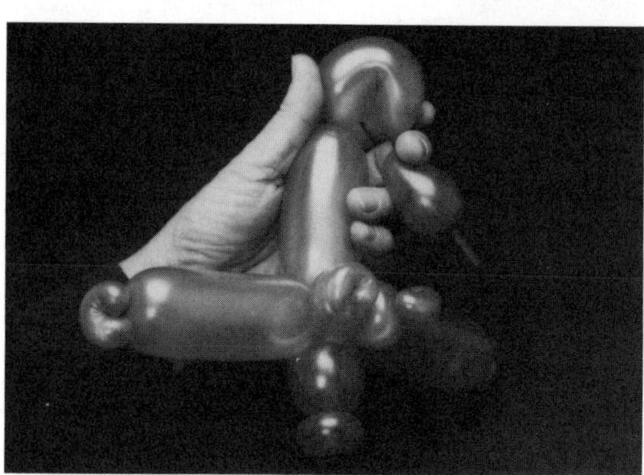

7 Form a 3-inch bubble for the body. To make the rudder, form a 2-inch loop and lock twist the ends.

8 To make one elevator, form a 1-inch loop and lock twist the ends.

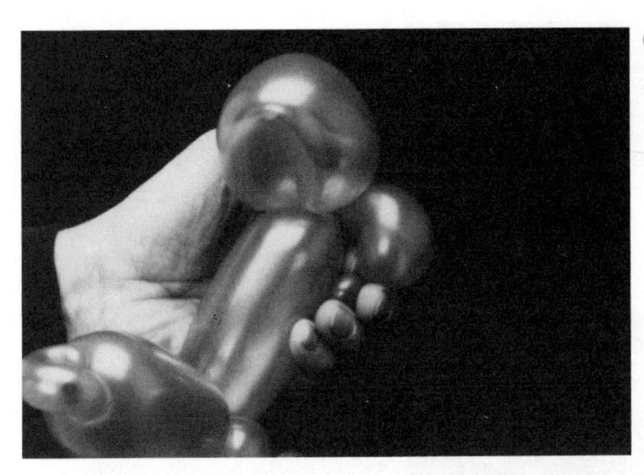

9. To make the other elevator, form a second 1-inch loop and lock twist the ends, twisting them at least four times. Remove the rest of the balloon by popping it.

10 Pinch twist the first and last ½-inch bubbles of the landing gear assembly, twisting each at least four times. Pop the second ½-inch bubble to separate the landing gear and complete the figure.

BIPLANE

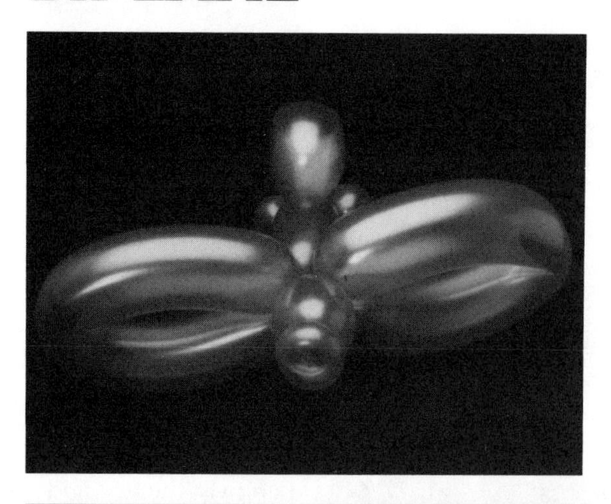

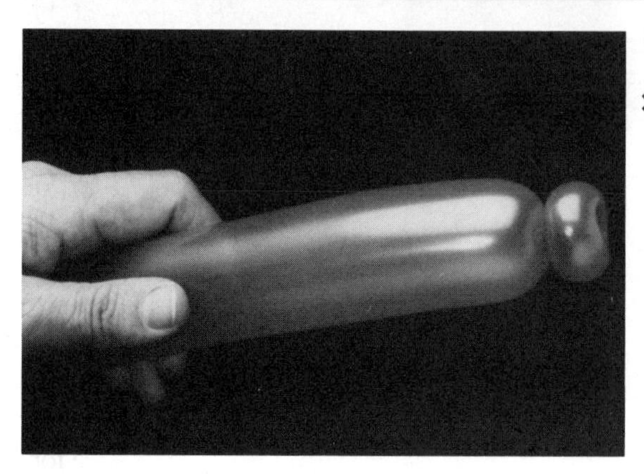

1 Inflate the balloon, leaving a 6-inch uninflated end. Tie a knot. Hold the balloon in your left hand with the uninflated end pointing left. Form a ½-inch tulip twist at the knot end to make the propeller.

2 Hold the tulip twist in your left hand with the uninflated end pointing right. Form a 1-inch bubble for the fuselage. To make the wings for one side, form a 5-inch loop and lock twist the ends.

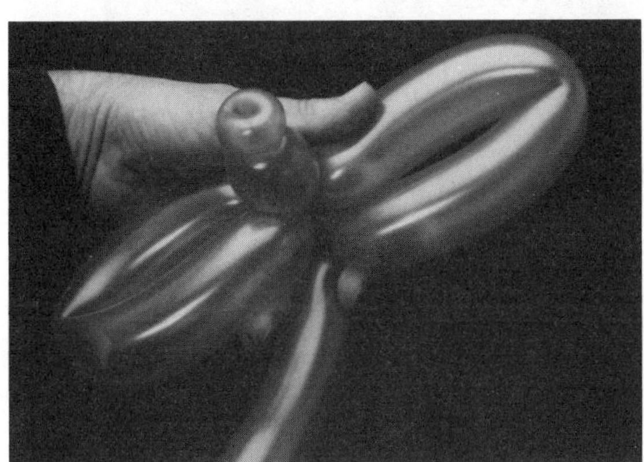

3 To make the wings on the other side, form a 5-inch loop and lock twist the ends.

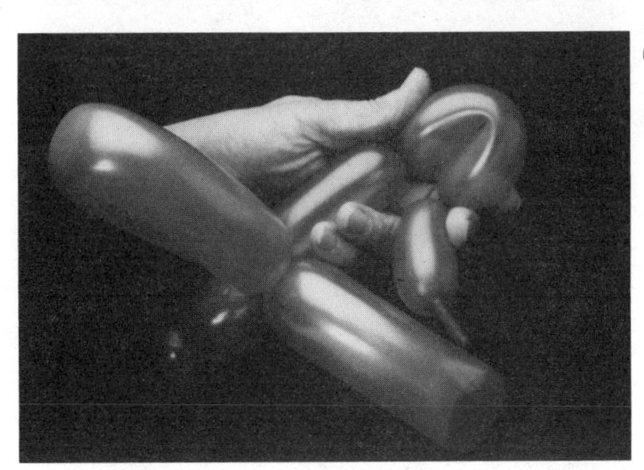

4 Form a 3-inch bubble for the body. To make the rudder, form a 2-inch loop and lock twist the ends.

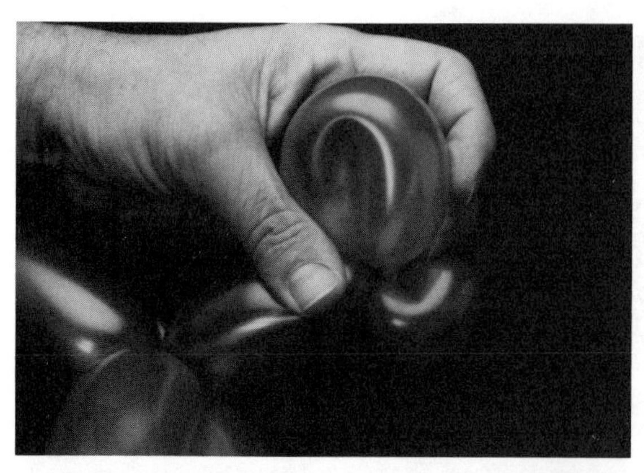

5 To make one elevator, form a 1-inch loop and lock twist the ends.

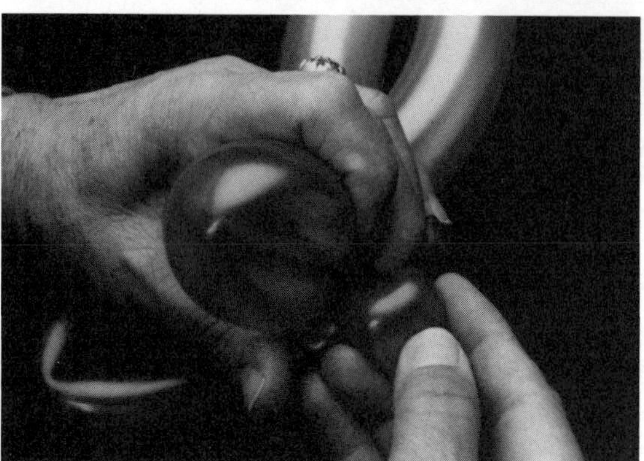

6 To make the other elevator, form a second 1-inch loop and lock twist the ends, twisting them at least five times. Remove the remainder of the uninflated end by popping it to complete the figure.

727 JET

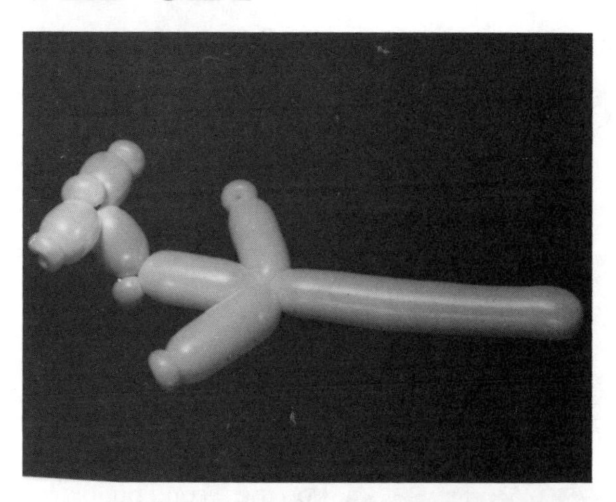

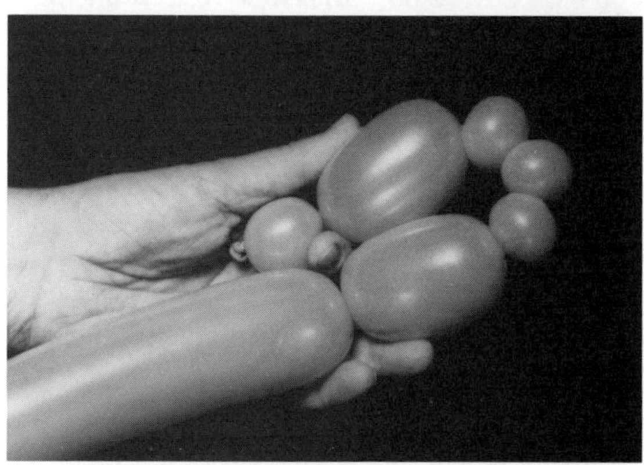

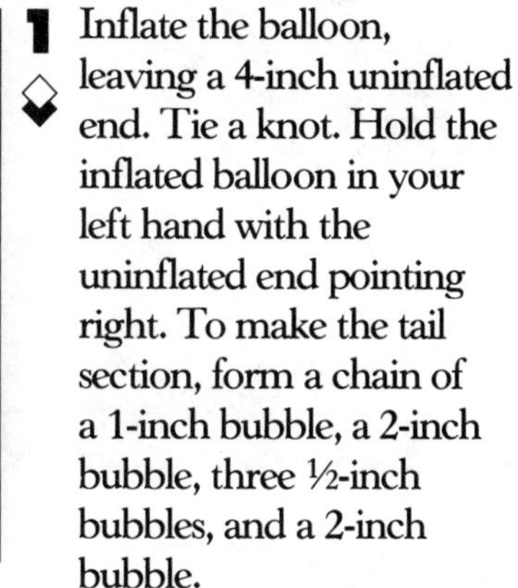

1 Inflate the balloon, leaving a 4-inch uninflated end. Tie a knot. Hold the inflated balloon in your left hand with the uninflated end pointing right. To make the tail section, form a chain of a 1-inch bubble, a 2-inch bubble, three ½-inch bubbles, and a 2-inch bubble.

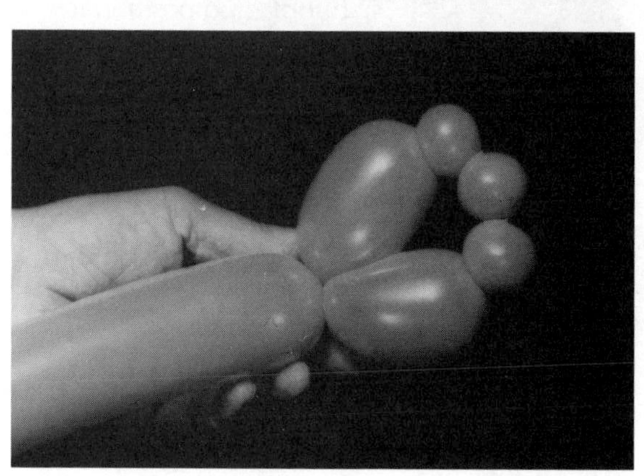

2 Lock twist the two 2-inch bubbles together at the base.

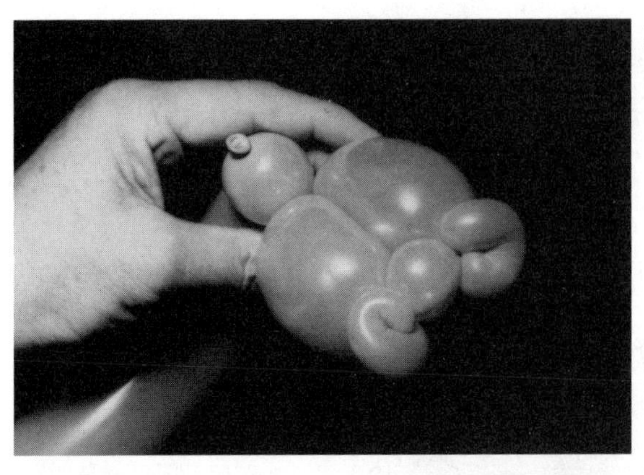

3 Pinch twist the first and last ½-inch bubbles, twisting each several times.

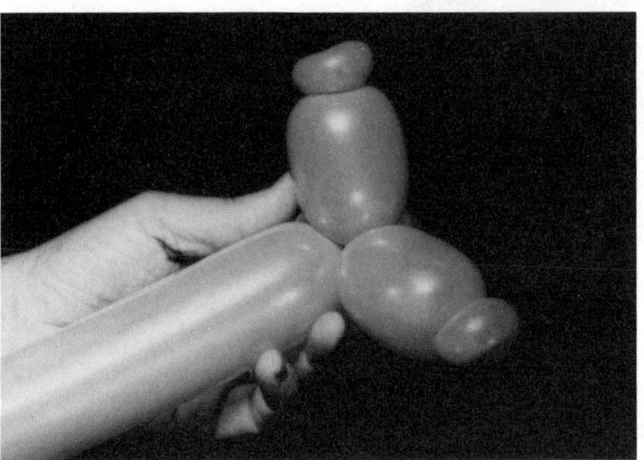

4 Pop the second bubble in the chain to separate the elevators.

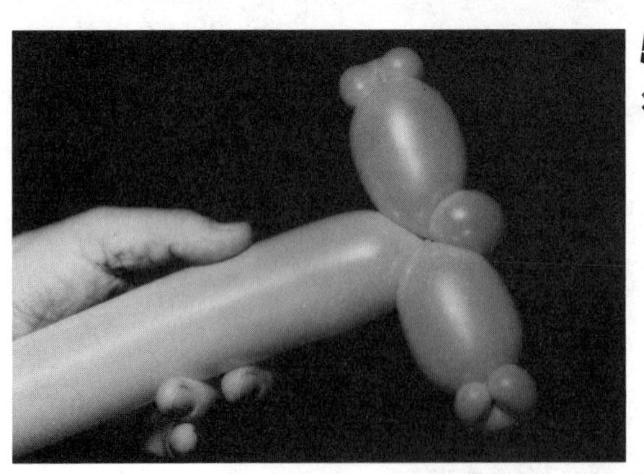

5 Pinch twist the 1-inch bubble and position it between the two elevators to hold them in a horizontal position and complete the tail section. The rest of the balloon should extend in the opposite direction.

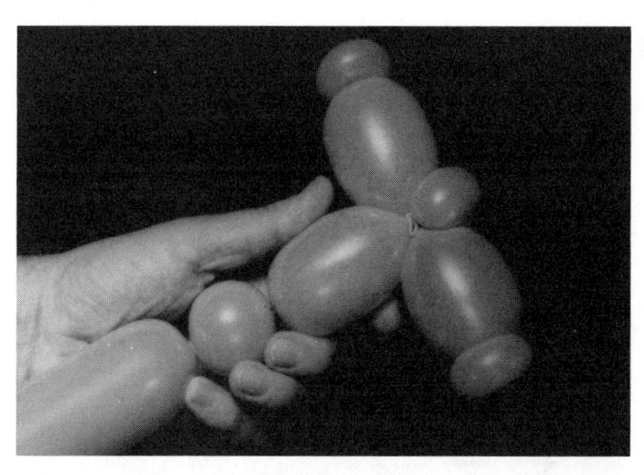

6 Form a 2-inch bubble for the rudder, then a 1-inch bubble.

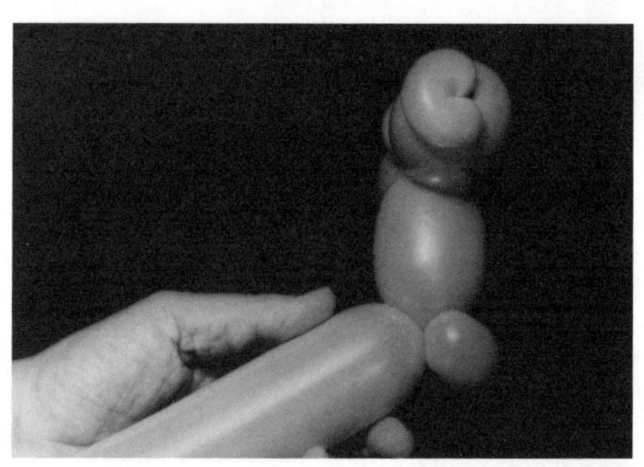

7 To hold the rudder and tail section upright, pinch twist the 1-inch bubble.

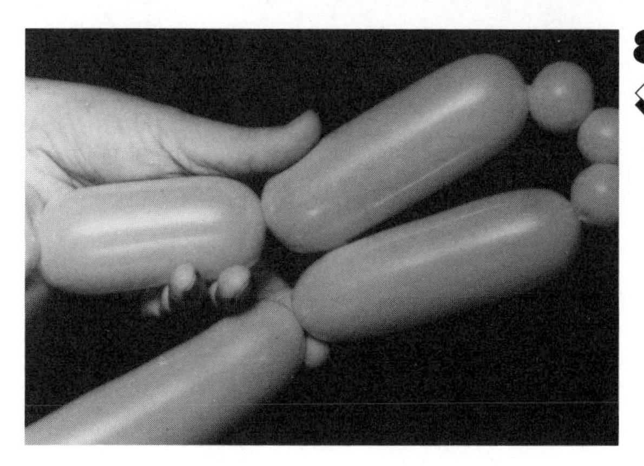

8 Form a 3-inch bubble for the rear fuselage. To make the wings, form a five-bubble pinch and pop series with a 4-inch bubble, three ½-inch bubbles and another 4-inch bubble.

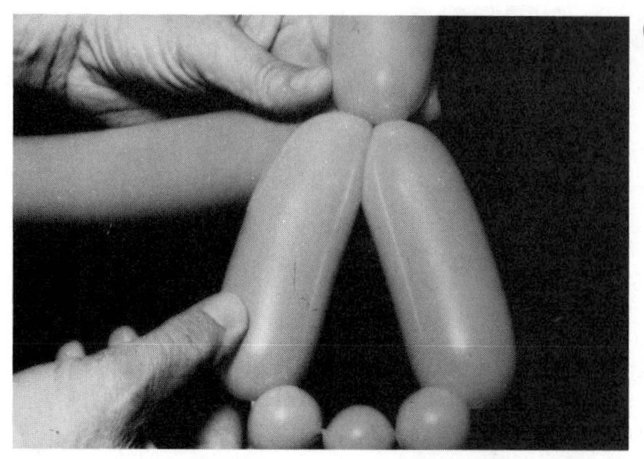

9 Lock twist the two 4-inch bubbles together at the base.

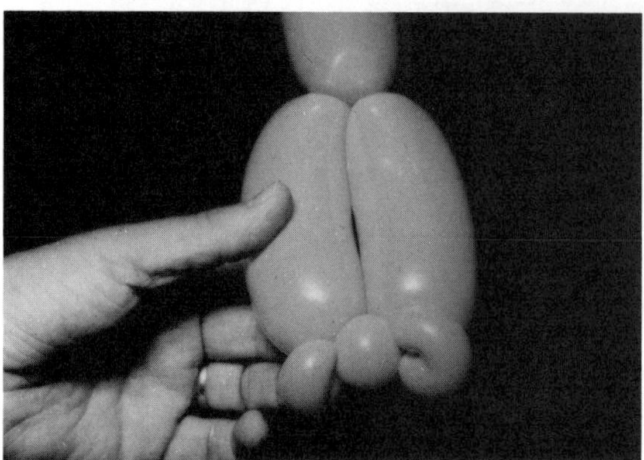

10 Pinch twist the first and last ½-inch bubbles, twisting each several times.

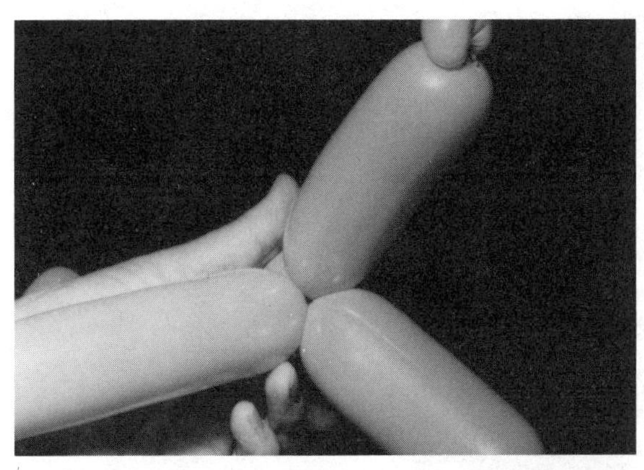

11 Pop the second ½-inch bubble to separate the wings.

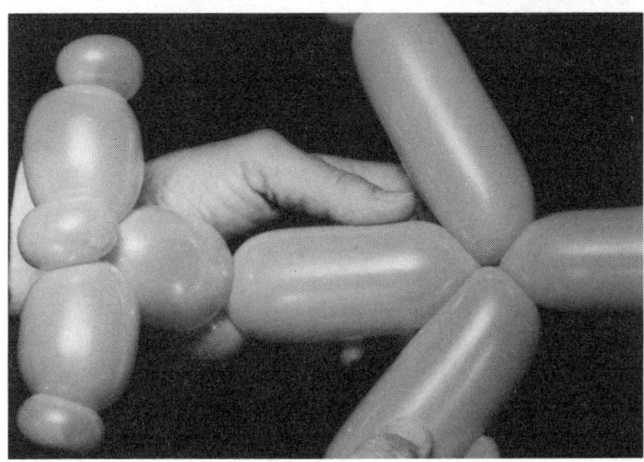

12 Position the wings so they slant toward the tail section to complete the figure.

THREE-BLADED HELICOPTER

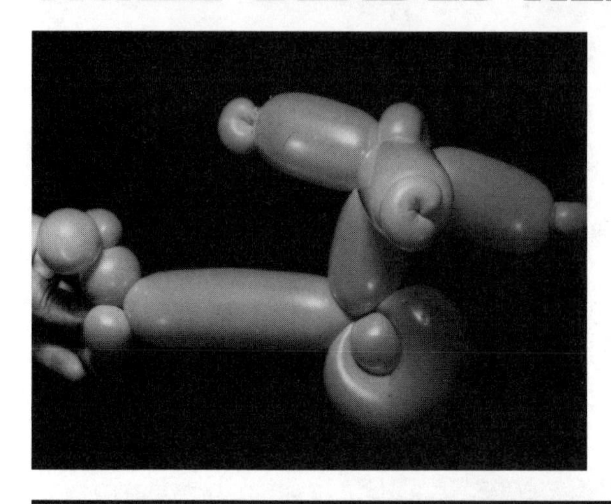

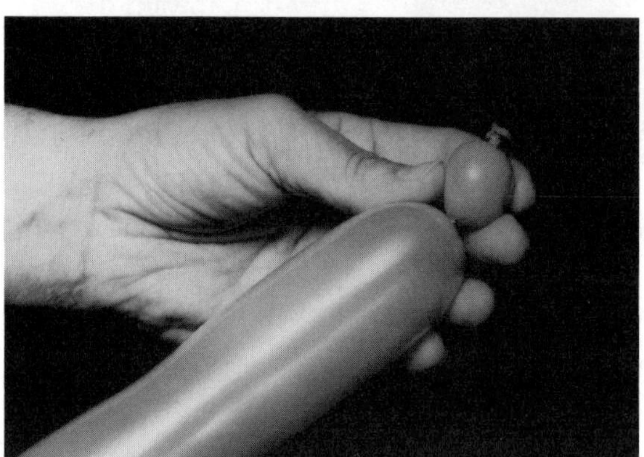

1 Inflate the balloon, leaving a 6-inch uninflated end. Tie a knot. Hold the balloon in your left hand with the uninflated end pointing right. To make the first rotor blade, form a ½-inch bubble at the knot end of the balloon.

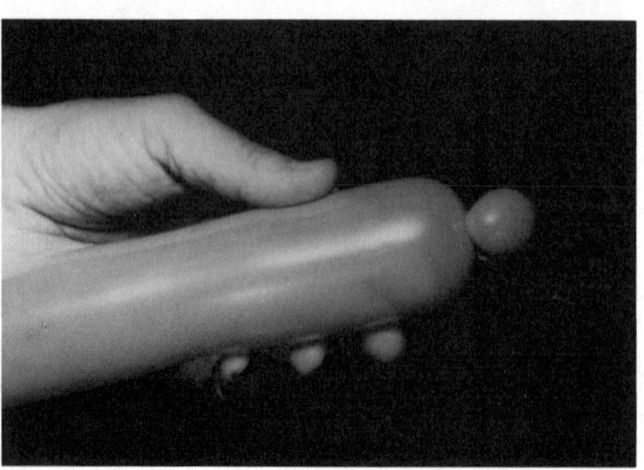

2 Pinch twist this bubble, then form a 3-inch bubble to complete the blade.

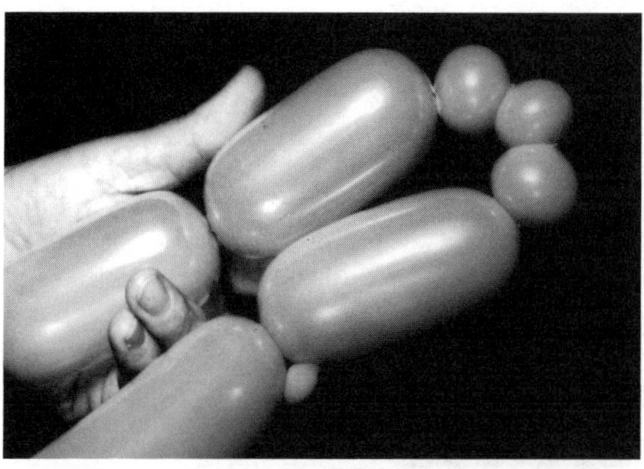

3 To make the other rotor blades, form a five-bubble pinch and pop series with a 3-inch bubble, three ½-inch bubbles, and a 3-inch bubble.

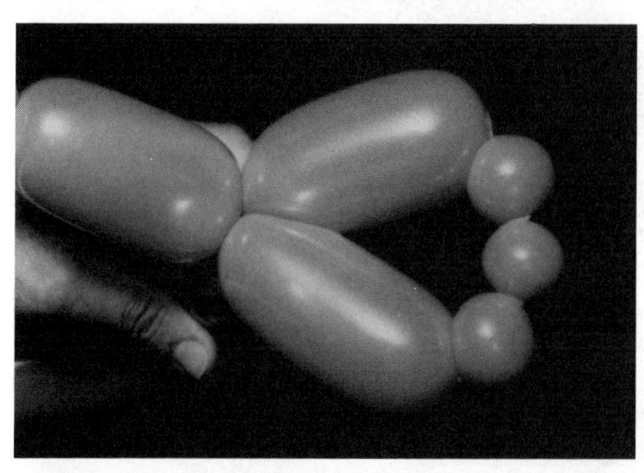

4 Lock twist the last two 3-inch bubbles at the base.

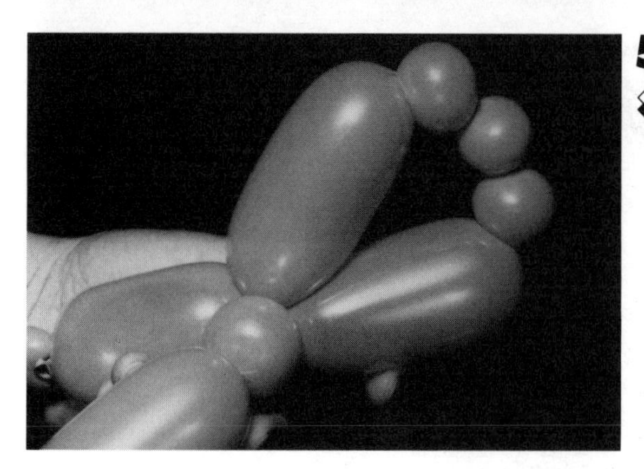

5 Form a 1-inch bubble and pinch twist it.

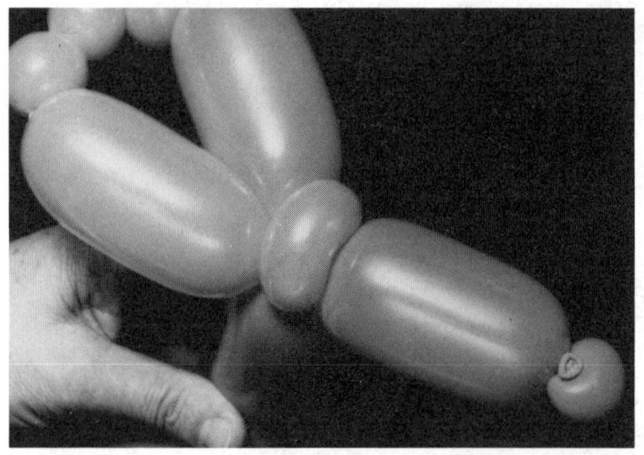

6 Position this pinch-twisted bubble where the three 3-inch bubbles meet and opposite the uninflated portion of the balloon so it rests on top of the finished blades.

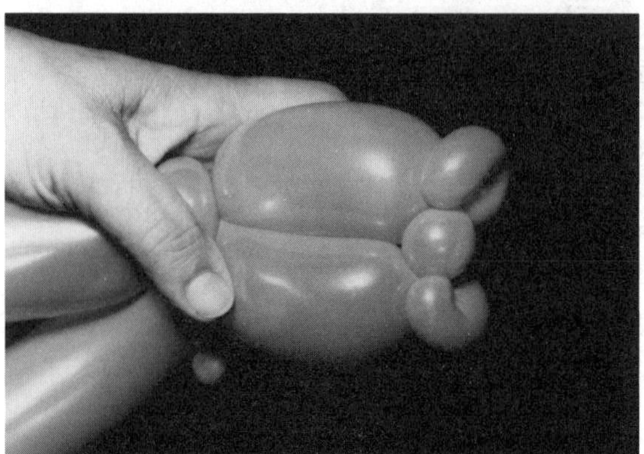

7 To complete the blades, pinch twist the first and third ½-inch bubbles, twisting each several times.

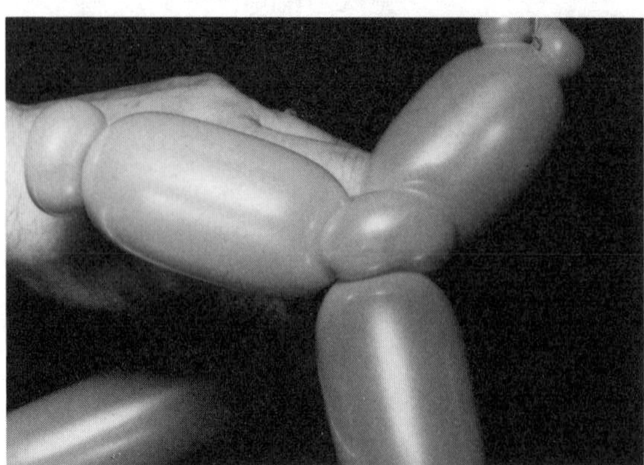

8 Pop the second ½-inch bubble to separate the second and third rotor blades.

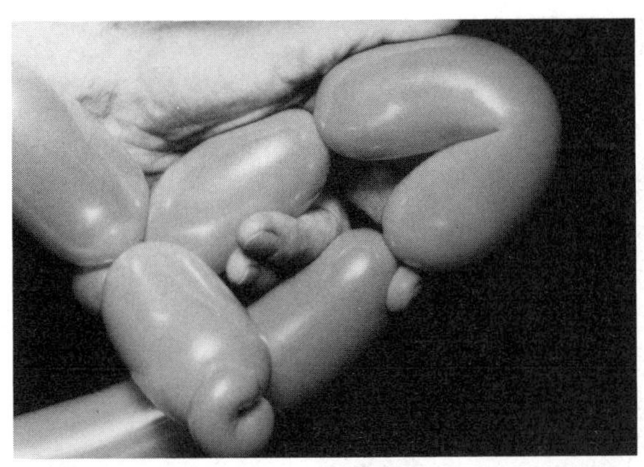

9 Form a 2-inch bubble for the upright, and a 2-inch loop for the cockpit.

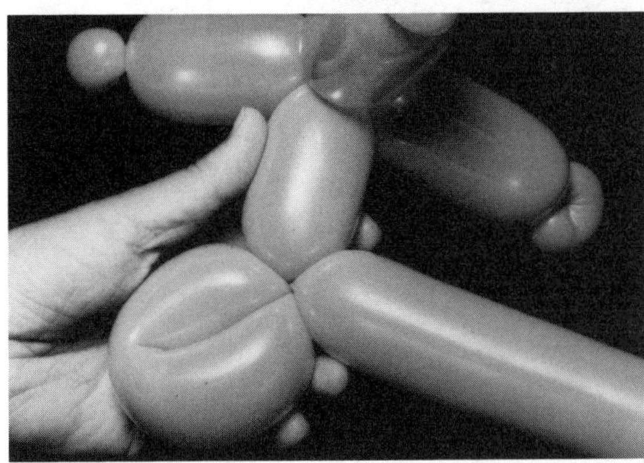

10 Lock twist the ends of the 2-inch loop.

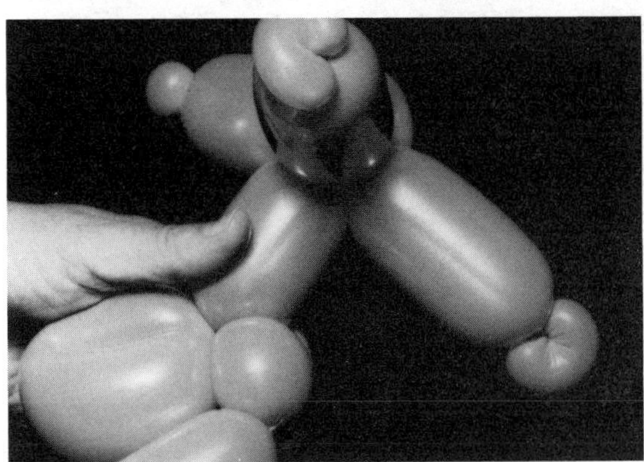

11 Form a 1-inch bubble.

12 Pinch twist this bubble and tuck it into the middle of the 2-inch loop to complete the cockpit.

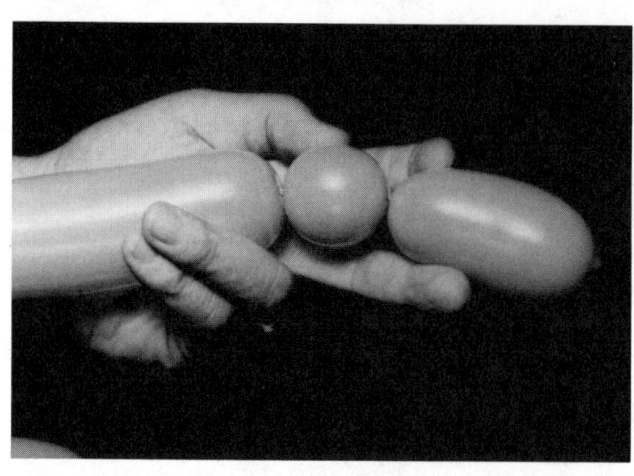

13 Form a 4-inch bubble for the tail frame, then a 1-inch bubble.

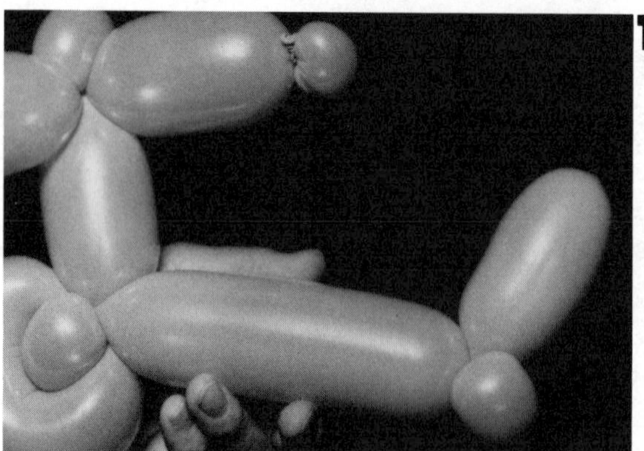

14 Pinch twist the 1-inch bubble and position it so it holds the tail section upward.

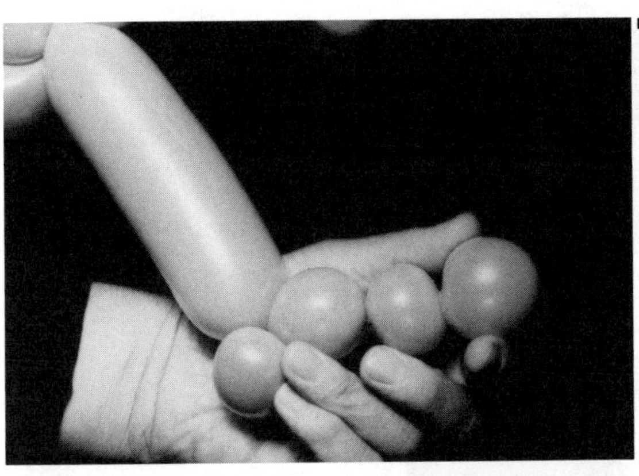

15 Form two 1-inch bubbles.

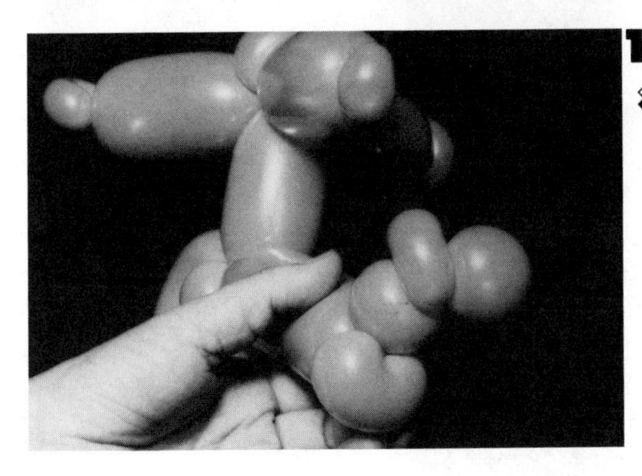

16 Pinch twist the second 1-inch bubble and position it so it turns the rest of the balloon to the side to make the stabilizer propeller and complete the figure.

SNOOPY

1 Inflate the balloon, leaving an 8-inch uninflated end. Tie a knot. Hold the balloon in your left hand with the uninflated end pointing right. To begin the figure, form an "S" shape in your left hand with about 6 inches of the inflated portion of the balloon.

2 Squeeze a small amount of air out of this portion and twist the balloon at the end of the "S." Then release the "S."

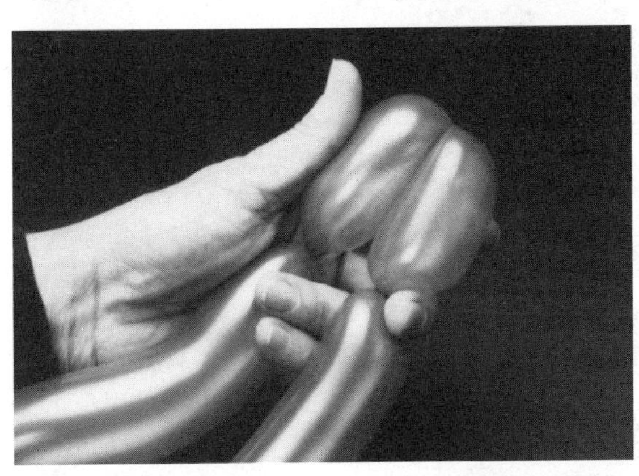

3 To make the ears, form two 1½-inch bubbles and lock twist them at the base.

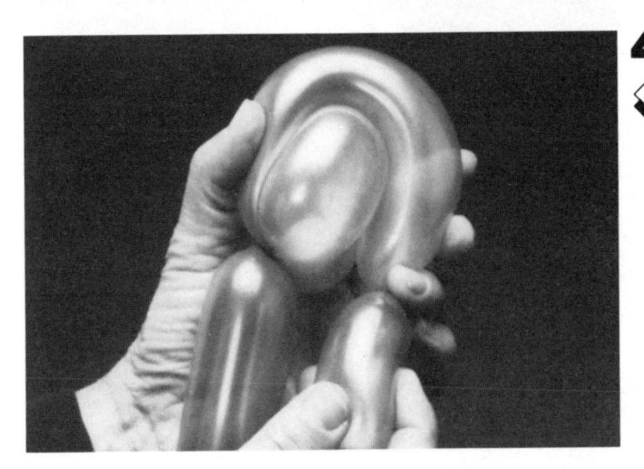

4 To make the head, form a 1½-inch bubble at the knot end of the balloon. Wrap the rest of the "S" around the ears formed in the previous step. Lock twist the single 1½-inch bubble with the base of the ears.

5 Form a 1-inch bubble for the neck. To make the front legs, form two 1½-inch bubbles and lock twist them at the base.

6 Form a 2-inch bubble for the body. To make the back legs, form two 1½-inch bubbles and lock twist them at the base. Leave a small bubble of air at the base of the tail to hold the back legs in place and complete the figure.

WOODSTOCK

1 Inflate the balloon, leaving a 6-inch uninflated end. Tie a knot. Hold the balloon in your left hand, with the uninflated end pointing right. Form a 1-inch bubble for the beak and a chain of seven ½-inch bubbles.

2 Form two 1½-inch bubbles at the end of the seven-bubble chain and lock twist them at the base.

3 To make the head and complete the beak, wrap the seven-bubble chain around the two 1½-inch bubbles. Lock twist the 1-inch bubble formed in step one with the two 1½-inch bubbles at the base.

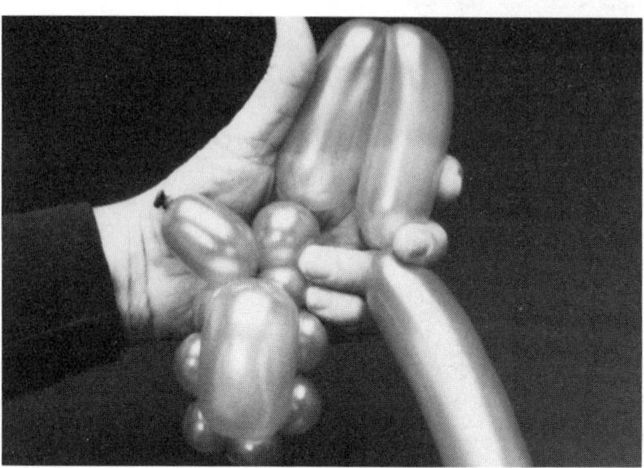

4 Form a 1-inch bubble for the neck. To begin the body, form two 3-inch bubbles.

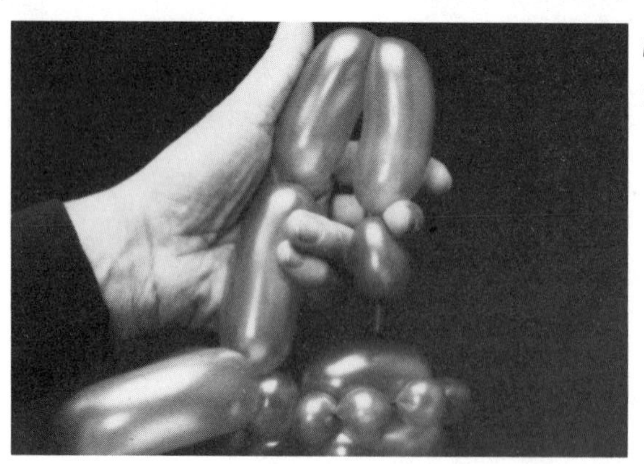

5 To make the legs, form a 3-inch bubble and two 2-inch bubbles. Lock twist the two 2-inch bubbles at the base.

6 Hold the single 3-inch bubble alongside the two 3-inch bubbles formed in step four.

7 Roll the two 3-inch bubbles over the single 3-inch bubble, while pushing the single 3-inch bubble between them to complete the figure.

DOLL

1 Inflate the balloon, leaving an 8-inch uninflated end. Tie a knot. Hold the balloon in your left hand with the uninflated end pointing right. To make the head, form a ¾-inch bubble and a 1½-inch loop. Lock twist the ends of the loop.

2 Tuck the ¾-inch bubble inside the 1½-inch loop to complete the head.

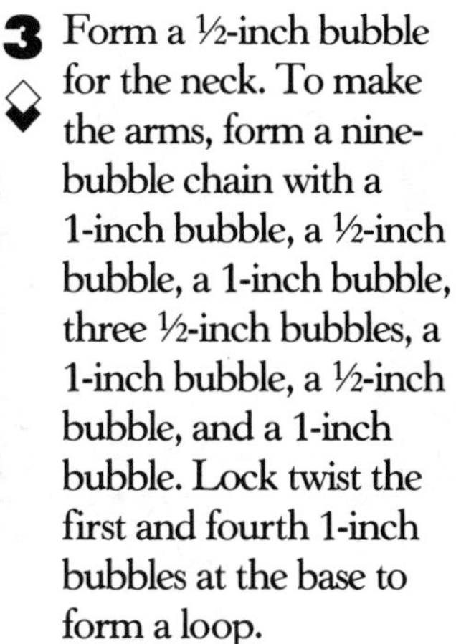

3 Form a ½-inch bubble for the neck. To make the arms, form a nine-bubble chain with a 1-inch bubble, a ½-inch bubble, a 1-inch bubble, three ½-inch bubbles, a 1-inch bubble, a ½-inch bubble, and a 1-inch bubble. Lock twist the first and fourth 1-inch bubbles at the base to form a loop.

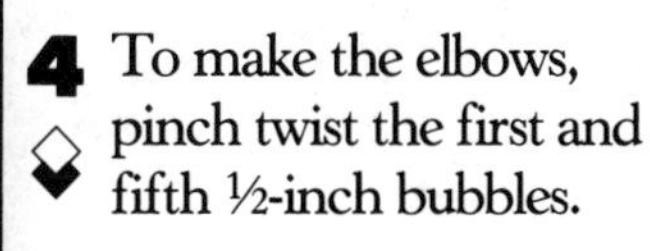

4 To make the elbows, pinch twist the first and fifth ½-inch bubbles.

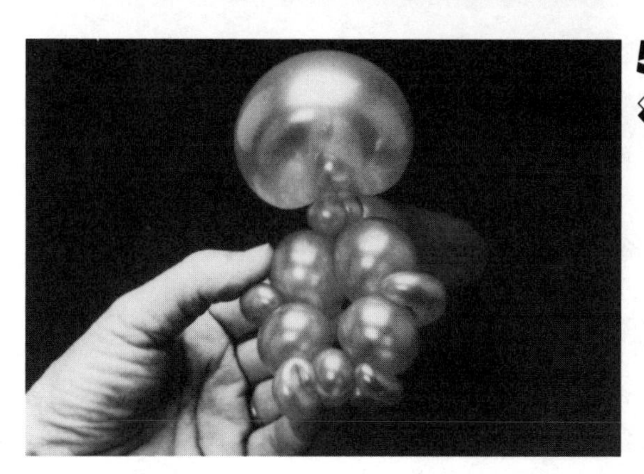

5 To make the hands, pinch twist the second and fourth ½-inch bubbles, twisting each bubble at least four times.

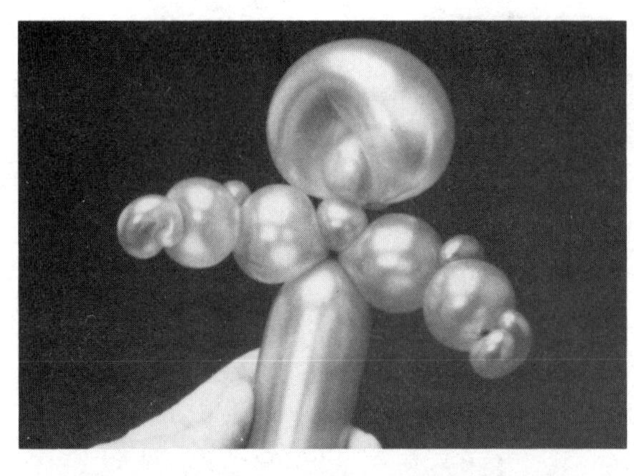

6 Pop the third ½-inch bubble to separate the arms.

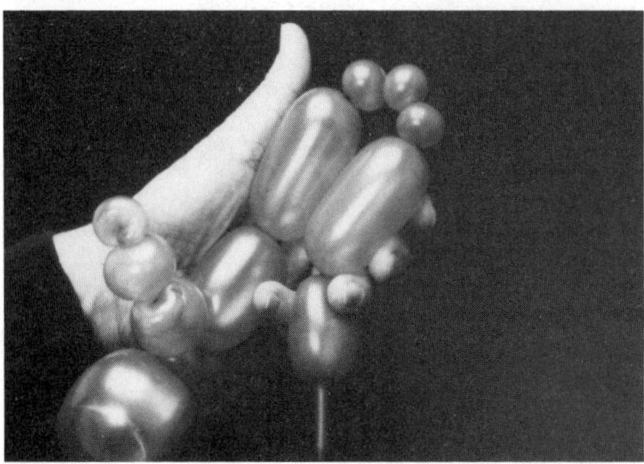

7 Form a 1½-inch bubble for the body. To make the legs, form a five-bubble pinch and pop series with a 2-inch bubble, three ½-inch bubbles, and a 2-inch bubble. Lock twist the 2-inch bubbles at the base.

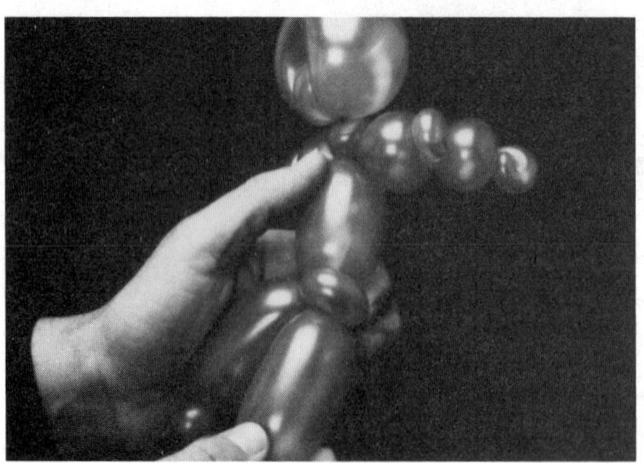

8 To make one hip, form a ½-inch bubble and pinch twist it.

9 To make the other hip, form a second ½-inch bubble and pinch twist it, twisting it at least four times. Pop the rest of the balloon to remove it.

10 To make the feet, pinch twist the first and last ½-inch bubbles of the legs. Pop the second ½-inch bubble to separate the legs and complete the figure.

ST. BERNARD

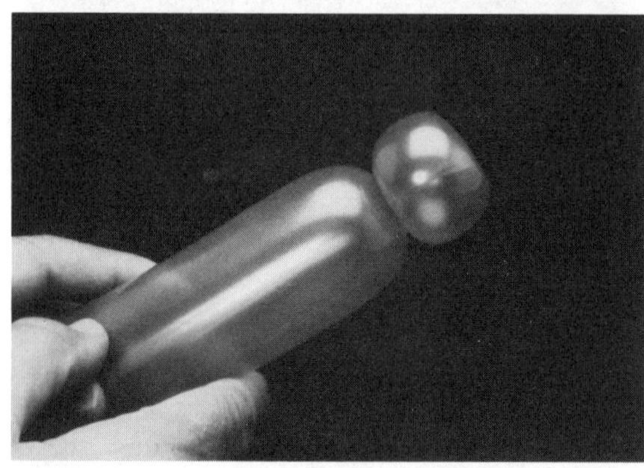

1 Inflate the balloon, leaving a 6-inch uninflated end. Tie a knot. Hold the balloon in your left hand with the uninflated end pointing left. Form a 1-inch tulip twist at the knot end of the balloon.

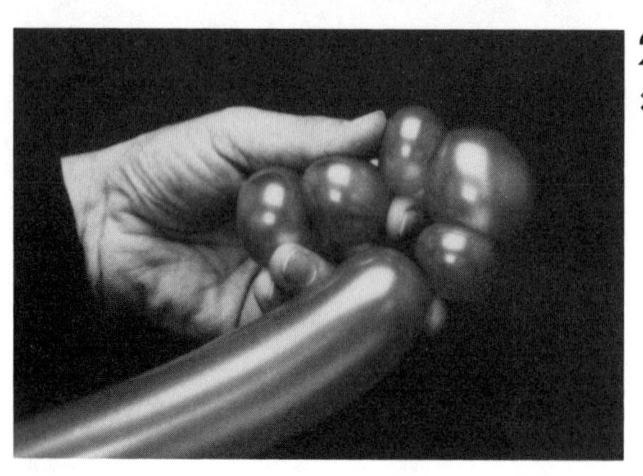

2 Hold the balloon in your left hand with the uninflated end pointing right. To make the head, form a chain of a 1-inch bubble, a ¾-inch bubble, a 1½-inch bubble, and a ¾-inch bubble. Lock twist the two ¾-inch bubbles at the base.

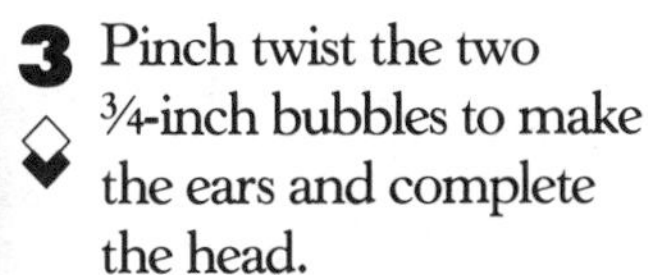

3 Pinch twist the two ¾-inch bubbles to make the ears and complete the head.

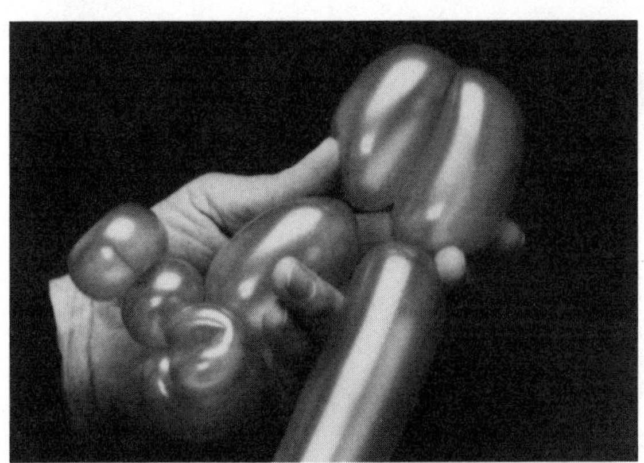

4 Form a 1½-inch bubble for the neck. To make the front legs, form two 1½-inch bubbles and lock twist them at the base.

5 To begin the body, form two 3-inch bubbles and lock twist them at the base.

6 Form another 3-inch bubble and hold it alongside the two-bubble lock twist formed in the previous step.

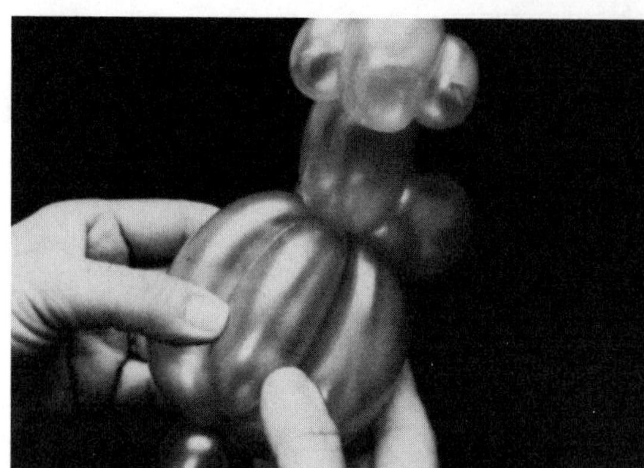

7 Roll the two 3-inch bubbles over the single 3-inch bubble while pushing the single 3-inch bubble between them to complete the body.

8 To make the back legs, form two 1½-inch bubbles and lock twist them at the base.

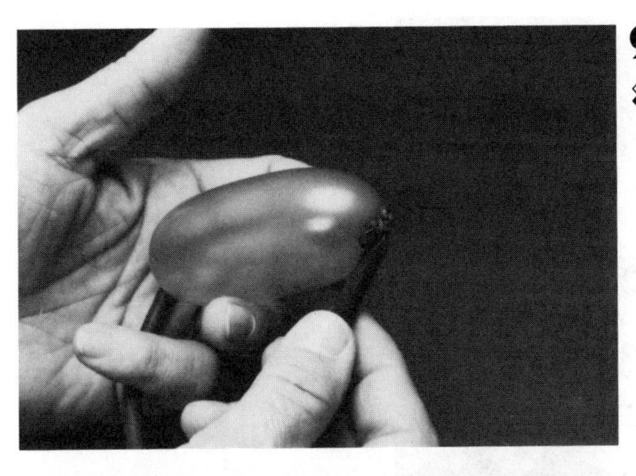

9 To make the keg, take a second balloon and inflate it to form a 2-inch bubble. Tie a knot. Tie together the uninflated end and the knot end.

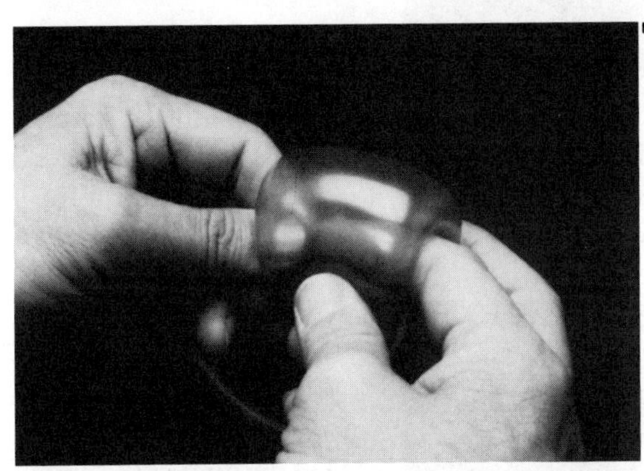

10 Tuck the knot formed above through the inflated portion of the balloon, then form a tulip twist with the uninflated portion of the balloon forming a loop.

11 Place this loop over the head of the figure to represent a brandy (or root beer) keg and complete the figure.

INFLATING IN THE MIDDLE

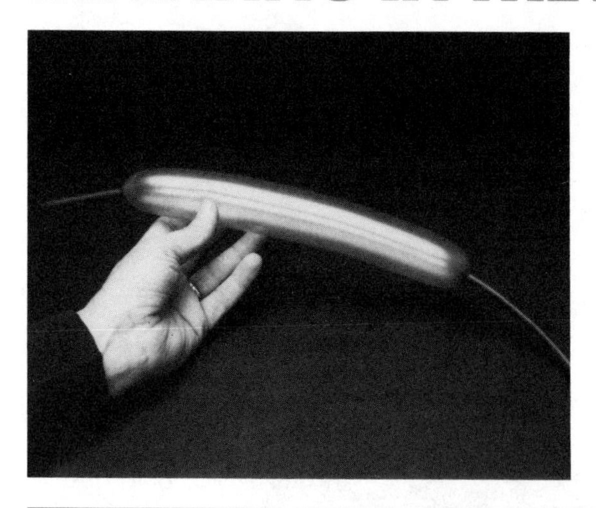

A number of detailed figures can be formed that require an uninflated portion at both ends of the balloon. The trunk of the elephant, the tail of the unicorn, and the kickstand of the motorcycle, for example, are all details formed at the uninflated lip (knot) end of the balloon.

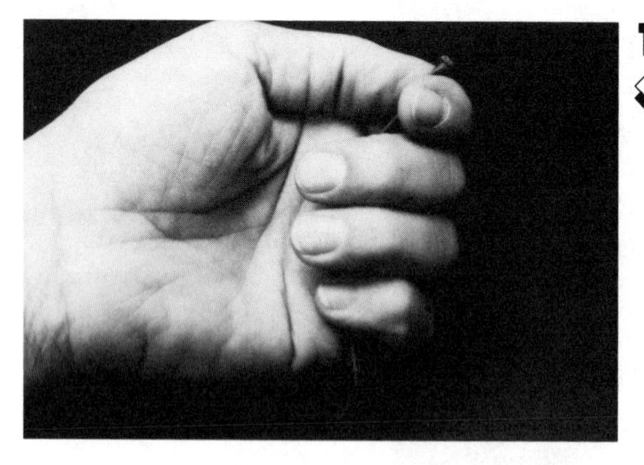

1 While inflating the balloon, hold a portion of it inside your hand to prevent it from expanding. Tie the knot at the end of the balloon (unless otherwise stated) as you continue to hold it.

ELEPHANT

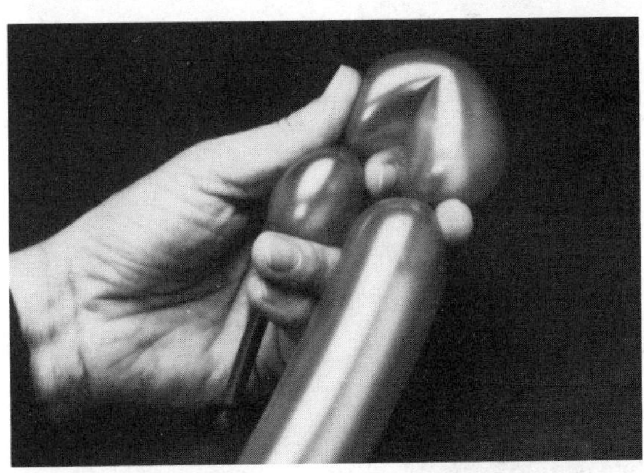

1 Inflate the balloon, keeping 3 inches uninflated at the lip end, and 4 inches uninflated at the opposite end. Tie a knot. Form a 1-inch bubble next to the uninflated portion at the lip (knot) end for the head. To make one ear, form a 1½-inch loop and lock twist the ends.

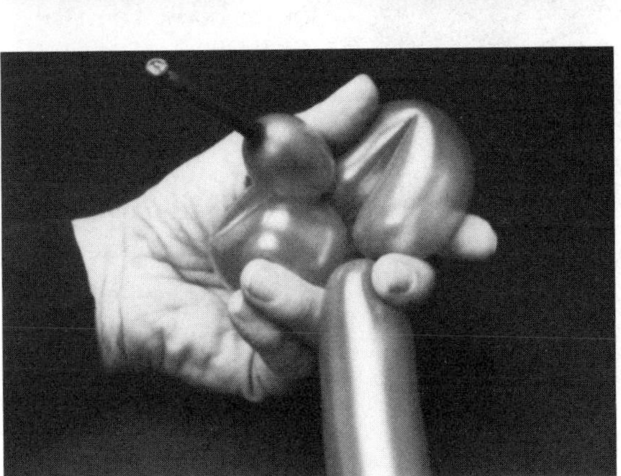

2 To make the other ear, form a 1½-inch loop and lock twist the ends.

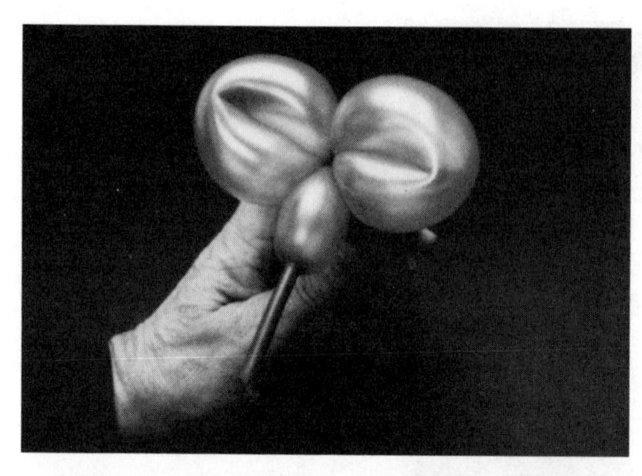

3 Position the head and trunk between the ears, as shown.

4 Form a 1-inch bubble for the neck. To make the front legs, form two 1-inch bubbles and lock twist them at the base.

5 Form a 2-inch bubble for the body. To make the back legs, form two 1-inch bubbles and lock twist them at the base. Form a small bubble of air at the base of the tail to hold the back legs in place and complete the figure.

UNICORN

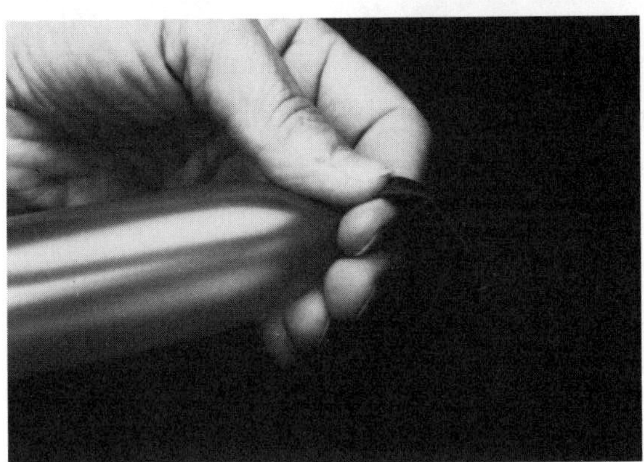

1 Inflate the balloon, keeping 1 inch uninflated at the lip (knot) end and 6 inches uninflated at the opposite end. Tie the knot next to the inflated portion of the balloon (not at the end). This "loose" end forms the tail.

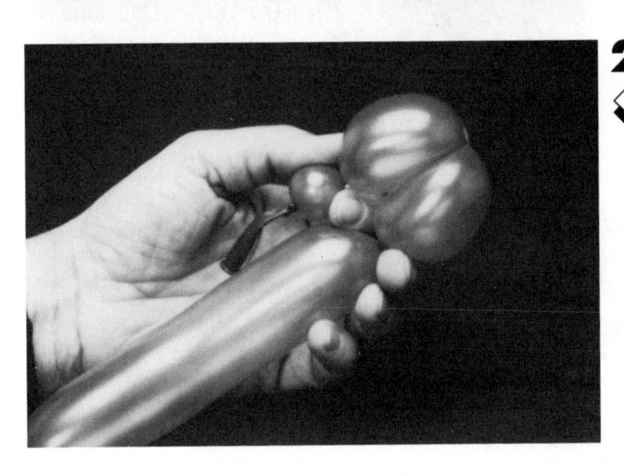

2 Form a ½-inch bubble next to the knot. To make the back legs, form two 1½-inch bubbles and lock twist them at the base.

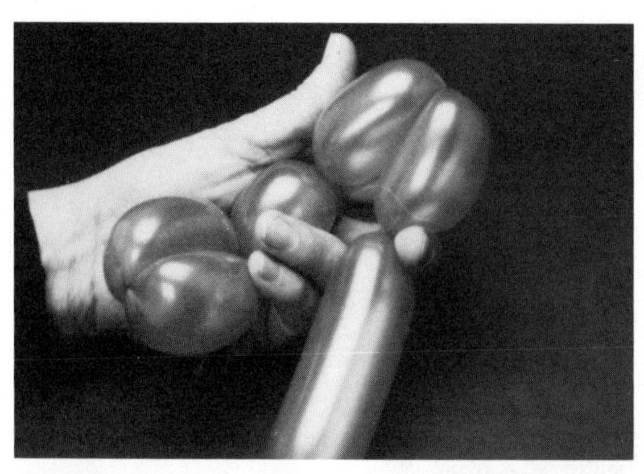

3 Form a 1½-inch bubble for the body. To make the front legs, form two 1½-inch bubbles and lock twist them at the base.

4 To make the mane, form a chain of six ½-inch bubbles. Lock twist the first and last ½-inch bubbles at the base.

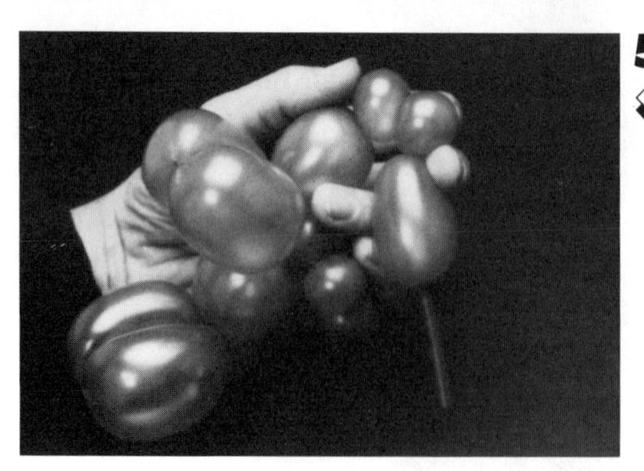

5 Form a 1½-inch bubble for the neck. To make the ears, form two ½-inch bubbles and lock twist them at the base.

6 To position the mane, stretch the six-bubble loop over the ears, wedging the ears between the third and fourth ½-inch bubbles of the chain.

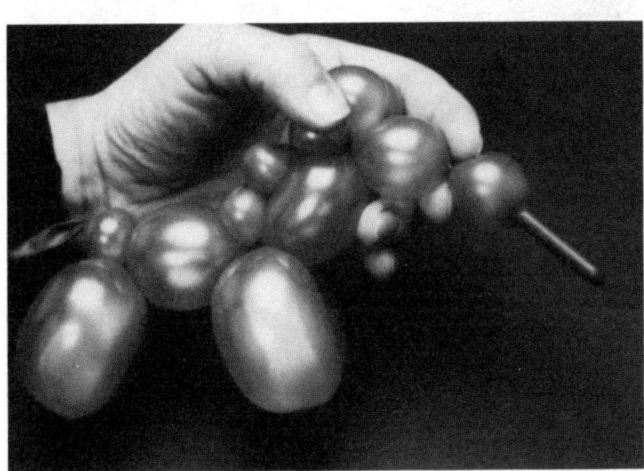

7 Twist the remaining inflated portion of the balloon in half.

8 Tie the uninflated tip of the balloon around the last twist to make the horn and complete the figure.

MOTORCYCLE WITH A KICKSTAND

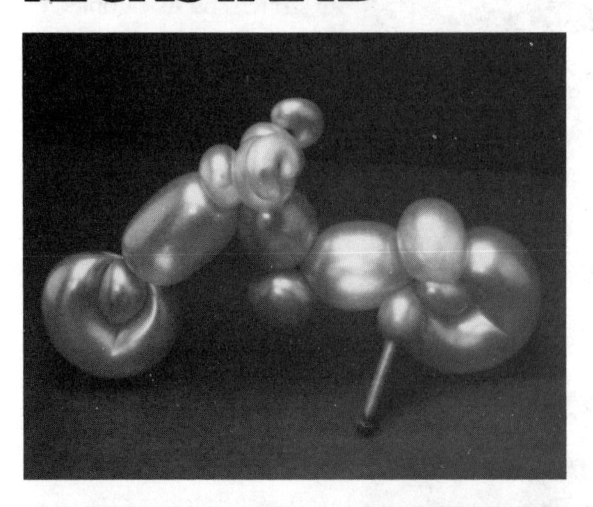

1 Inflate the balloon, keeping 2 inches uninflated at the lip (knot) end and 6 inches uninflated at the opposite end. Tie a knot.

2 Form a ½-inch bubble next to the uninflated lip (knot) end. To make the back wheel, form a 1½-inch loop and lock twist the ends.

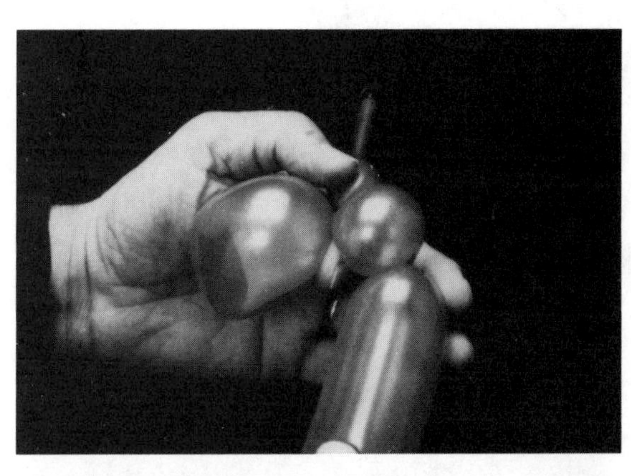

3 Form a 1-inch bubble.

4 Pinch twist this bubble and tuck it inside the center of the 1½-inch loop to complete the back wheel.

5 To make the seat and hold the rear wheel in position, form a 1-inch loop and lock twist the ends. Make sure the uninflated lip end is on the left side of the rear wheel.

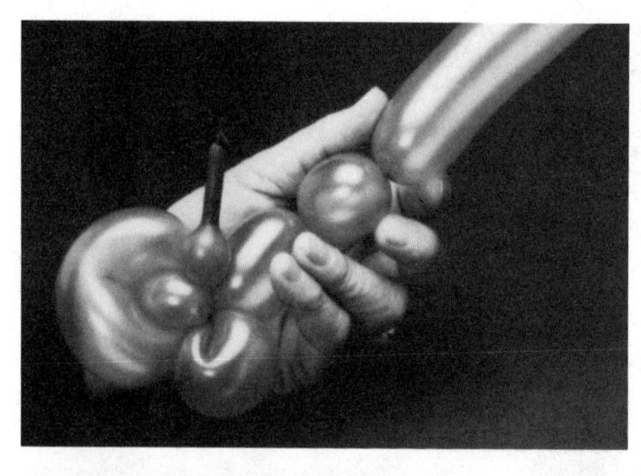

6 Form a 1½-inch bubble for the frame, then a 1-inch bubble.

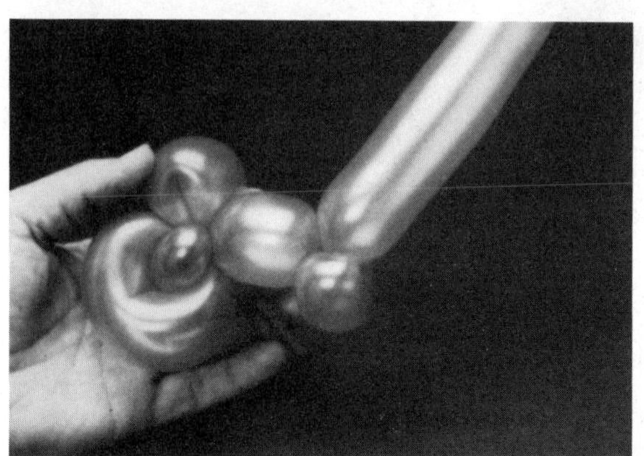

7 Pinch twist the 1-inch bubble to make the motor.

8 Form a 1-inch bubble for the upright. To make the handlebars, form a five-bubble pinch and pop series with a ¾-inch bubble, three ½-inch bubbles, and a ¾-inch bubble. Lock twist the two ¾-inch bubbles at the base.

9 Form a 1-inch bubble. Pinch twist this bubble in front of the handlebars to hold them in proper position.

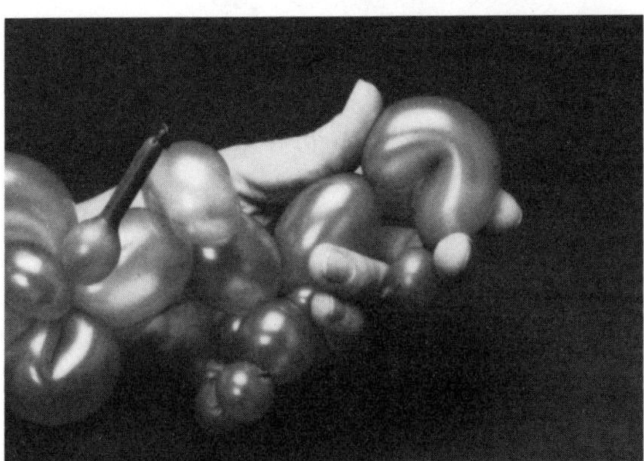

10 Form a 2-inch bubble for the front forks. To make the front wheel, form a 1½-inch loop and lock twist the ends. Tuck the rest of the balloon inside the center of the 1½-inch loop to complete the front wheel.

11 Pinch twist the first and third ½-inch bubbles of the handlebar assembly, twisting each bubble at least four times. Pop the second ½-inch bubble to separate the handlebars and complete the figure.

INDEX

About the Author, 203
Adding Detail, 14
Airplane, 158
Alligator, 120
Antlers, 29
Basic Animal, 6
Basic Loop Figure, 21
Basic Twists
  Lock, 4
  Two-Bubble, 5
Bassett Hound, 16
Bicycle, 154
Biplane, 162
Bouquet, 59
Bullfrog, 126
Bunny Rabbit, 12
Cat, 23
Chihuahua, 64
Chopper, 150
Dachshund, 18
Daisy, 52
Deer, 30
Doll, 182
Dove, 104
Eagle, 108
Elephant, 191
Elk, 32
Fish, 130
Five-Bubble Series with
  Pinch and Pop, 85
Five-Bubble Series with
  Pinch Twists, 83
Floppy Ears, 14
Four-Bubble Twist, 40
Frog, 123
Giraffe, 10
Headphones, 141
Helicopter, Three-Bladed, 170
Horse, 73
Inflating, 2
Inflating in
  the Middle, 190
Jet (727), 165
Kangaroo, 69
Kissing Fish, 132
Lamb, 81
Lion, 79
Lock Twist, 4
Loop Twist, 20
Loop and Tuck, 39
Love Birds, 94
Love Birds
  in a Swing, 97
Mane, 72
Monkey, 45
Moose, 34
Motorcycle with
  Kickstand, 196
Mouse, 8
Orchid, 54
Parrot in a Swing, 101
Pinch Twist, 61
Pistol, 139

Poodle, 41
Poodle with Ears, 43
Proportion, 7
Ram/Bighorn Sheep, 36
Road Runner, 115
Rocking Horse, 76
St. Bernard, 186
Scooter, 147
Skateboard, 144
Ski Pole, 137
Snoopy, 176
Squirrel, 66
Sunflower, 56
Swan, 26
Sword, 135
Teddy Bear, 87
Teddy Bear on
  a Unicycle, 90
Three-Bubble Series with
  Pinch Twists, 63
Three-Bubble
  Roll Through, 93
Tulip, 50
Tulip Twist, 48
Turkey, 111
Turtle, 118
Twists
  Five-Bubble Series
    with Pinch
      and Pop, 85
    with Pinch
      Twists, 83
  Four-Bubble, 40
  Lock, 4
  Loop, 20
  Loop and Tuck, 39
  Pinch, 61
  Three-Bubble
    Roll Through, 93
  Three-Bubble Series
    with Pinch, 63
  Tulip, 48
  Two-Bubble, 5
Two-Bubble Twist, 5
Tying, 3
Unicorn, 193
Woodstock, 179

ABOUT THE AUTHOR

Internationally known magician Marvin L. Hardy has been delighting audiences with his talent for more than 35 years – while also earning for himself the title of the world's foremost authority on balloon sculpture. His repertoire of balloon figures is virtually limitless, including scores of familiar animals, celebrity caricatures, and phenomenally intricate one-balloon creations that astonish even fellow balloon artists.

Hardy is so enthusiastic about the art and its applications that he has developed a complete, instructional balloon figure-tying kit. He eagerly shares his skills with others, including the handicapped and elderly, through workshops and seminars. Balloon magic, he believes, is an art form that's as entertaining to watch as it is to create.

At home before groups of any size, Hardy is noted both for his outstanding showmanship and the instant rapport he develops with those he entertains. He travels extensively around the United States, promoting and performing magic and balloon art.